MW00953228

CAN I SAY A PRAYER WITH YOU?

A BEGINNER'S GUIDE TO PRAYING WITH SOMEONE

Father David Scotchie

Uramado Press

CAN I SAY A PRAYER WITH YOU?
A BEGINNER'S GUIDE TO PRAYING WITH SOMEONE

For information:
Father David Scotchie
Most Precious Blood Catholic Church
113 Lockwood Boulevard
Oviedo, FL 32765
407-365-3231
frdavidscotchie@gmail.com
Facebook: www.facebook.com/frdavidscotchie

Illustrations: Mary Doerfler Dall
Cover Image: Theresa Degler
Book Layout: Tim Schoenbachler
Photo: Janeth A. Bejarano

First Printing: December 2016

TABLE OF CONTENTS

Introduction 7

HOW DO YOU PRAY WITH SOMEONE?....................... 15

SCRIPTURE SHOWS US HOW TO PRAY FOR OTHERS .. 47

THE SAINTS SHOW US HOW TO PRAY FOR OTHERS... 67

HOW DO YOU ASK SOMEONE TO PRAY FOR YOU? 91

WHAT YOU CAN SAY ABOUT SUFFERING 109

Conclusion 139

Resources for Your Prayer Life 145

Acknowledgments 151

Endnotes 153

DEDICATION

To my brother priests

INTRODUCTION

Once I made a retreat in Sedalia, Colorado. The retreat center was on a hill. A path wandered along the rim of the hill and gave great views of the Rocky Mountains to the west and the city of Denver to the north. I liked to walk the path through the grassy lawns. The retreat grounds were like a park, green and quiet, dotted with trees.

The Stations of the Cross ran along the path. Every twenty steps or so, a granite monument depicted a moment along the way of the cross from Jesus' trial to his crucifixion and death. The stations started at a statue of Jesus kneeling before the cross. It portrayed the Garden of Gethsemane.

Jesus went with his disciples to the Garden of Gethsemane after their Passover meal. Telling his closest companions, Peter, James and John, that his soul was sorrowful even to death, he asked them to stay near and keep watch. He fell to the ground and, anticipating his certain arrest, trial and crucifixion, he prayed, "Abba, Father, take this cup away from me, but not what I will but what you will" (Mark 14:36).

Three times Jesus returned to Peter, James and John and each time he found them asleep. He chastised them for taking their rest while he was in agony. "Could you not keep watch for one hour? The spirit is willing but the flesh is weak" (Mark 14:37-38). The one thing Jesus wanted in the Garden was a few friends to pray with him![1]

What happened next would bring anyone to their knees. Judas, one of his own twelve apostles, would lead a mob armed with swords and clubs into the garden. He would kiss Jesus as a sign. The crowd would seize him and haul him before the chief priests and elders and scribes for a show trial before his fated crucifixion.

Gazing on the Gethsemane scene at the retreat center, something occurred to me. Just as Jesus prayed in the garden to his Father, even now he was praying in heaven to his Father!

I had always pictured the risen Christ seated in heaven at the right hand of the Father, sharing in his reign. Works of art painted on cathedral ceilings show the royal Jesus. It was not hard to get the idea that the risen Christ was in heaven clothed with glory and power.

With the kneeling Jesus before me, I realized that he was not just seated in heaven. He was doing more than simply gazing in glory upon the cosmos waiting to come again to judge the living and the dead.

At the beginning of Mass, the priest leads the people in the Penitential Act. "Brothers and sisters, let us acknowledge our sins, and so prepare ourselves to celebrate the sacred mysteries."

After a brief pause for silence, the priest invokes the Lord Jesus, "You are seated at the right hand of the Father to intercede for us."

The people acclaim, "Lord, have mercy."

Jesus is not just sitting on his heavenly throne. He is interceding for us. He is praying on our behalf.

The Letter to the Hebrews tells us that Jesus is the Great High Priest. As did the temple priests of old, he mediates between God the Father and his people. Risen from the dead and ascended into heaven, he now appears before God on our behalf (Hebrews 9:24).

Jesus is the Lamb of God who takes away the sins of the world. His sacrifice on the cross sets us free from sin. It makes us free for him. By the blood of his sacrifice, we are washed clean.

At the same time, he is the royal high priest who offers his own self as sacrifice to God the Father. "Because he has a priesthood that does not pass away, he is always able to save those who approach God through him, since he lives forever to make intercession for them" (Hebrews 7:24-25).

While I was standing in the retreat center garden, looking at the statue of Jesus kneeling before the cross, Jesus was at the right hand of the Father, making intercession for you and me. Every moment of every day, he is interceding for us.

Because the risen Christ is a priest interceding for us at the right hand of God the Father, we can pray, "... through Christ our Lord." This ending is not tacked on to the end of every prayer as a pious way to say, "... and now our prayer is over." It means that we direct our prayer to God the Father through Christ. He is praying for us. He is talking with God the Father on our behalf. Our prayer to God "through Christ our Lord" is joining with his prayer for us.[2]

We take to heart the familiar question, "What would Jesus do?" Jesus proclaimed the kingdom of God, so we likewise talk about God and how much he loves us. As Jesus forgave sinners, we offer his pardon and his peace. We do what Jesus did.

Here's where the penny dropped. As Jesus prays for us, we can pray for others. Besides asking, "What would Jesus do?" we can ask, "What would Jesus pray?" WWJP is just as sure a guide as WWJD.

I am an ordained priest. I am conformed in a special way to Christ, the Great High Priest, through the Sacrament of Holy Orders.

But everyone who has received the Sacrament of Baptism shares in Christ's priestly identity. The Book of Revelation says that Christ "has made us into a kingdom, priests for his God and Father" (Revelations 1:6). All who are baptized share in his priesthood. The baptized have the responsibility and authority to pray for others.

The first letter of Peter, recalling the promise that God made to the Israelites on Mount Sinai, tells us that "you are 'a chosen race, a royal priesthood, a holy nation, a people of his own, so that you may announce the praises' of him who called you out of darkness into his wonderful light" (1 Peter 2:9). Mingling politics and religion, the mixed metaphor "a royal priesthood" describes who we are before God. We are mediators before God on behalf of those in darkness.

This short book is for you who are ready to take to heart WWJP. It assumes no special training or knowledge of the Bible. It does not assume a devout prayer life. You do not need to have had visions of heaven.

All that you need is the desire to help others. These reflections and stories direct your desire to help others become prayer for others and prayer with others. It guides you to follow Jesus who even now is praying for you.

The first chapter, "How Do You Pray with Someone?", gives you practical tips and examples of people praying with patients, children, strangers, and friends. It helps you to consider that you do not have to be an ordained priest to pray with someone. You might fear looking foolish, but love casts out all fear.

The second chapter, "Scripture Shows Us How to Pray for Others," is to set aside concern that praying with others is an innovation not integral to our faith. The four men on the roof lowering a paralytic before Jesus and Abraham walking and talking with the Lord over the fate of Sodom are two scripture stories of the power of prayer.

The third chapter, "The Saints Show Us How to Pray for Others," encourages you to look to the saints. They model how to ask for help. As your friends in high places, they are more than ready to pray with you.

Padre Pio, Maximilian Kolbe, and other saints inspire us to pray.

The fourth chapter, "How to Ask Someone to Pray with You," is leading by example. Pope Francis, at the announcement in St. Peter's Plaza of his election to the papacy, bowed his head in silence while the hundreds of thousands of the faithful prayed for him. If the pope can ask someone to pray for him, so can we. When we step forward to pray with others, we need prayers for ourselves more than ever.

The final chapter, "What You Can Say about Suffering," wrestles with the tough questions just below the surface. Why is there suffering at all? Why do bad things happen to good people? What is God doing about suffering? When you pray with someone who is suffering, they may need to talk about the meaning of their suffering. The chapter helps you consider what you might say to someone about their sufferings.

The book is titled, *Can I Say a Prayer with You?* It's one thing to say, "I'll say a prayer for you." Praying for others is a good thing. It's a powerful prayer, though, that prays with someone on the spot.

Rather than wait until the end of the day when you say your bedtime prayers, why not pray with someone when the moment arises? Can you imagine Jesus saying to someone, "I'll pray for you," and then walking away? Neither can I.

Jesus prayed with the sick, the sinful, and the hurting. When Jesus prayed with them, they became better. They were helped. They moved from sickness to health, from darkness to light, from death to life.

For their sake, let's do what Jesus does and pray with one another.

ONE

How Do You Pray with Someone?

It Helps to Be a Priest. Even So...

One day I was throwing the Frisbee for my dog Maxie. We were at the parish church where I was the pastor. I wandered over to a man who was standing nearby. He was a contractor who was doing some work on our parish campus. He was waiting for his co-worker to arrive.

The contractor and I talked about dogs. He told me how he had grown up with a house full of beagles.

Seeing my collar, he told me that he had attended Catholic primary school in Orlando years and years ago and even had been an altar server. Although he attended a Methodist church with his Protestant wife, he quoted his elderly mother whom he looked after. "Once a Catholic, always a Catholic."

We talked some more about the weather and whatever. Making ready to continue my stroll, I decided to introduce myself properly, "I'm the pastor, Fr. David. What's your name?"

"Joe. Nice to meet you," as we shook hands.[3]

I took a leap of faith. "Can I say a prayer with you?"

"Sure," he shrugged behind his sunglasses. "Why not?"

"What do you want to pray for?"

He smiled. "The usual – world peace."

"Anything in particular?"

"My mother, she's getting old."

"Okay, then."

I folded my hands and bowed my head, "Lord, bless Joe and his family. Take care of him as he takes care of his mother. Amen."

We shook hands and I returned to the parish office and the day's cares. That was that, I thought.

That afternoon, not one but two parishioners related separately to me that Joe could not say enough about meeting their pastor Father David. He did not tell them about my dog Maxie and her Frisbee tricks. He did not talk about his contract work for us.

He told two people that I had prayed for him. A simple invitation to pray had made a difference to Joe.

My encounter with Joe was not unusual. After Mass, people ask me to pray for a sick cousin in Puerto Rico, their family leaving on a trip, or perhaps for themselves going through a tough time. Rather than say, "Sure, I'll keep you in my prayers," I've learned over the years to pray with parishioners on the spot.

Praying with them now rather than later is practical. I am simply not able to remember later on for whom I'm supposed to pray. I become busy with other things and forget. While a general prayer at the end of the day for the people I have promised to pray for is good, I want to be sure that I really do pray for them.

Praying with them on the spot makes the prayer personal. I ask the name of the sick cousin. If I don't know the name of the parishioner, my memory loss becomes an opportunity. "I'm sorry, can you help me with your name again?"

Sometimes I grab a little old church lady walking by and ask her to pray with us. Little old church ladies might not know who we are praying for, but they know the power of prayer. Where two or three are gathered together, Christ is with us. There is strength in numbers.

My prayer is usually as simple as my prayer with Joe the contractor. "Lord, bless N. and his family. Take care of his cousin and heal him. Amen."

When I chat with people in my office or bless their home, I might ask them, "What do you want to pray for?" In the airport, rather than stare at my smartphone, I might strike up a conversation and offer to say a prayer.

My opening is evident. I am a priest. People see my collar and expect me to say something like, "Can I say a prayer with you?"

How do you who are not a priest get up the courage to ask, "Can I say a prayer with you?" How do you go about it? How do you pray with someone else?

In this chapter, I make several suggestions. I offer a number of examples to show how real people who are not a priest have stepped up and asked, "Can I say a prayer with you?" First, you have to face your fear.

Face Your Fear of Looking Foolish

When she was eighteen years old, Sister Briege McKenna developed rheumatoid arthritis. She could walk only painfully and slowly. The doctors said she would eventually be confined to a wheelchair. The doctor gave her so much cortisone that it became ineffective. The pain was constant.

At the same time, Sister Briege wanted spiritual healing even more than physical healing. Saying her prayers came to her as a duty. She wanted to know the Lord, whatever it took.

It happened at a prayer meeting. Sister Briege had closed her eyes and simply said, "Jesus, please help me."

She had hardly said the words when she felt a hand touch her head. She thought it was the priest at the prayer meeting. She opened her eyes yet saw no one touching her.

There was a power going through her body. She felt like "a banana being peeled." Her stiff fingers became limber. Her sores on her elbows were gone. She could see that her feet in sandals were no longer deformed. She jumped up screaming, "Jesus! You're right here!"

Since that prayer meeting, Sister Briege has been free of rheumatoid arthritis and pain.[4]

This is not the place to wonder why some are healed and many more are not. I could tell you ten stories of no apparent healing for every story of healing. The wonder, though, is that there are indeed healings of body, soul and spirit.

Sister Briege McKenna has much to say about this in her book, *Miracles Do Happen*. But at first, she had nothing to say.

After her rheumatoid arthritis was miraculously cured, she did not talk about the healing. For months, she kept it to herself. She told herself that she did not want to give people false hope. The truth, though, was that she was afraid of what people might say if she talked about being healed.

The Lord had other plans. Six months later, she received the gift of healing. In prayer, a burning sensation went through her body as if she touched an electrical outlet.

She said, "Jesus I don't want any gift of healing. Keep it for yourself. I promise I'll never tell anybody about this." She did not want to be seen as a fool. She was afraid of her reputation.

Eventually the Lord changed all that. She became an instrument of the Lord's will to heal. She became instrumental to many healings, some physical and always spiritual. Healing, she says, is saying yes to God. It may or may not mean physical cures. It always means a deeper healing that destroys your sin and restores you to more abundant life.

What makes me smile is how Sister Briege fought tooth and nail against the healing power given to her by the Lord. Why did she not want the gift of healing? She was afraid of looking foolish. She would let someone suffer rather than risk a little embarrassment.

Who could have blamed Sister Briege? We are used to being competent. Before we take on a task, we want to be sure that we can do it well and meet others' expectations.

When I ask someone to consider being a teacher for faith formation, I get all sorts of questions. What is the time commitment? What knowledge of the faith is required? Are there trainings? What are the ages of the children? The potential catechist looks carefully through the family calendar and talks with his wife. Making a commitment to teach for twenty-eight weeks takes consideration.

Like a would-be catechist, we are slow to commit ourselves until we are sure that we can do the job right.

A book on change management gave three basic reasons why change in a business is so hard. The second reason given was the fear of failure. (The other two reasons were the failure to see the necessity for change and the failure to finish the change.)

An example of the paralyzing power of the fear of failure was Smith Corona. Started in 1887, the company had mastered the business of making typewriters. The name Smith Corona was synonymous with typewriters.

The company knew how to make typewriters. It did not know how to make keyboards for personal computers. When the personal computers began to appear in the 1980s, Smith Corona continued making typewriters. They added word processors to their product line but lost market share.

Smith Corona eventually went through two bankruptcies. Today it is a much smaller company that makes thermal labels and thermal transfer ribbons but no typewriters.

The fear of failure paralyzes businesses and individuals alike. For us who are used to being competent and respected, the fear of failure can make us hesitate to pray with someone. After all, praying with someone runs two great risks.

The first risk is that you pray with someone and nothing happens. You present yourself as able to help and you fail. You feel like a fool. Rather than let someone down, you do not even offer to pray with them.

The second risk is the opposite. You pray with someone and something does happen. They feel peace. They are given hope. A quiet strength blooms. They might tell you later that the situation you prayed for has changed for the better.

The risk with answered prayer is that it opens your door to the Holy Spirit. It challenges you to step out of your comfort zone. It may lead to changes in your life where you are not in control. When you see that prayer really works, you glimpse the loving power of the Holy Spirit.

For this to happen, you must face your fear of looking foolish. Ask yourself, "What's the worst thing that could happen if I dare ask, 'Can I say a prayer with you?'"

Then consider another way to look at praying with someone. Ask yourself, "What's the best thing that could happen if I dare ask, 'Can I say a prayer with you?'"

Like Sister Briege, pray with others. Miracles do happen.

PRAY WITH SOMEONE YOU LOVE

Offering to pray with someone is a scary thought. We don't like to look foolish. We don't care to be called a "Jesus nut." What if they say no? We don't want to go out on a limb and be left hanging.

What might push us to take the risk and offer a prayer is a desperate situation. When someone you love is in a bad way, you may be ready to try anything. You may even dare to say, "Let us say a prayer."

Wanda called me just before lunch. I was making a stew. I did not need her to say her name. Having been close to her family for some years, I knew Wanda's voice. It was full of panic. "We don't know where he is!"

"Thomas never showed up Monday for the closing of his new home. The past three days, his fiancée has not been able to reach him on his phone. The wedding was supposed to be tomorrow."

Not sure what I could do that the police could not, I grabbed the soup off the stove and put it in a cooler to keep it from spilling in the car. Maxie my dog jumped into my car and we headed to their home.

Bob, waiting for me at their door, took the handle of the cheap Styrofoam cooler. The handle tore loose from the Styrofoam. Half of the soup poured onto his front stoop.

For the moment, the crisis of Thomas was overtaken by the crisis of the soup. We laughed. Maxie helped Bob mop up the spilled soup. Enough stew had stayed in the pot for the three of us to sit down over lunch. Wanda filled me in about their son.

"The wedding was set for Friday. He and Carol were supposed to close on a home on Monday. He did not show up at the closing. He has not been at work all week. In fact, he had resigned from his teaching position at the beginning of the year. I have no idea what is going on."

I did what I normally did when I had no idea what to do. I said, "Let us say a prayer."

We held hands on the dining table and bowed our heads. "Lord, we don't know where Thomas is. His parents and sisters are really worried about him. His fiancée Carol is really worried about him. You, though, know where Thomas is. Keep him safe. Bring him home. We know you can do this because you raised Jesus from the dead. Through Christ our Lord. Amen."

We talked some more. I asked Bob and Wanda to let me know when they heard from Thomas.

The next day, Wanda called. Thomas had come home late last night exhausted but okay. He had gone straight to bed. In the morning, they talked.

It turned out that when he did not show up for the house closing, it was only the end of a long road that Thomas had been walking in secret.

For several years after college, he had lived at home while teaching at a local school. He had continued going to Mass with his parents but had never claimed his Catholic faith as his own.

"I could probably list the number of times I missed Mass on one hand plus a finger. My family made sure that we found a church even while on vacation. I went because my parents went and I wasn't really given a choice to stay home."

He had had a series of girlfriends. He was not involved in the Church in any way. His lack of an inner life eventually became his way of life.

"I snuck out of my parent's house to go live with another girlfriend. I packed all of my things into trash bags and left while they were out running errands. I left no note, no explanation."

He ignored his family. His emails were few and far between. During this time, the youngest of his dad's brothers died. Thomas saw the email about his uncle and ignored it. He kept his back turned on his family in their need. He stopped going to church.

Thomas became involved with a teacher at his school. He proposed to Carol on a trip to St. Augustine. Talking about their future, Carol made clear that their children would not attend Mass with him and would not be exposed to a "cult." Thomas agreed.

"In a few months we had booked a venue, flowers, a minister, and picked out my suit. We also decided to purchase a house. That was the next step right? But I wasn't truthful to her. I didn't have as much money as I made her believe. Then the bottom started to become nearer."

For several reasons, his temporary teaching certificate expired. Forced to resign his teaching position, he lied to his fiancée and his parents by getting up every morning and pretending to go to work. When Carol discovered his lie, they decided all the same to go ahead and close on the house and get married.

"The day of closing, I didn't have the money to close on the house or finish off the deposits of the wedding. I sold a few things to get enough cash to get a motel room so I wouldn't have to go home and face any of this. I turned off my phone and pawned it for a hundred dollars. No one could reach me or know my location."

Earlier in the week he had scoped out highways until he found a high overpass without protective fencing. Wednesday evening, Thomas went to a bar and drank until he couldn't see straight.

"We had learned as teachers to look for signs of suicide: thoughts, previous attempts, method, and the means to carry out the method. Check, check, check, and check again. I knew that I met the criteria."

Thomas had always been scared of heights. Step ladders, balconies, and even the tree house in the backyard had terrified him. He became drunk at the bar to overcome this fear. Even then, he hesitated. It was as if from birth God had given him the fear of heights for that moment on the overpass.

"I got out of my car and stood on the ledge. I looked over the edge. I got back in my car. I stepped out of the car and looked over the edge. I got back in my car. I did this numerous times. I couldn't take that last step. I even wrote my goodbye notes to my parents, sister, and my fiancée, and put them on my dashboard. I started to write a note to my nephew. He was only a month old. Then something happened.

"It was like a dream. I didn't see a face but I knew it was him, my nephew, as an adult. If I went through with it, I would not get to see him grow up. The thought made me stone-cold sober. And I began to weep."

That night Thomas slept in his car in his parents' neighborhood, unable to bring himself to pull into their driveway. He was close to home but not home yet. For the next morning, instead of going home, he went to find another bridge.

"That first overpass was done. But instead of driving to find another overpass, I drove to the local university. I did not know why. I found myself at the library and wondered if I was going to read a book. There was a computer. I typed an email to my mom, 'Can I come back home?'"

The hour when he went to the university, logged into his email, and wrote to his parents was the hour when his parents and I were praying for him around their dining room table. Our prayer together for him marked a turning point.

That night, the prodigal son came home. His parents welcomed him home with open arms and tears of thanks.

Thomas did not get married to Carol. He went back to church and, joining a Bible study, came to know some people in a real way without any secrets. A year to the day that he was supposed to be married, he gave his witness at a men's retreat. He was home.

As for me and the mother and father of Thomas, we were grateful that he was alive. We were glad that we had the chance to pray for him. Our prayers and the love of his family, including his one-month nephew, had saved his life. Miracles do happen!

PRAY FOR PATIENTS[5]

Suzette Boyette is a Nurse Practitioner in a medical practice for women's health. Celebration Obstetrics & Gynecology, near Orlando, is a busy practice. Suzette sees about one hundred women a week ranging in age from thirteen to ninety-two years old. She examines them, does pap smears and other procedures, gives diagnoses, and writes prescriptions. And a few times a week, when it is appropriate, she prays with her patients.

One patient complained of pain in her abdomen. She had had a total hysterectomy. Suzette's exam of the woman offered no ready reason for the pain. She ordered some tests to rule out the obvious. Not being in a great hurry, they started talking.

"It turned out that she was angry. Her older sister had been on dialysis. Growing tired of the burden, her older sister stopped going to dialysis and died. This happened about six months ago. The patient's pain had begun coincidentally about a month after her sister passed."

Suzette's patient was mad at her sister for giving up. As they talked, Suzette decided to make a suggestion.

"Tonight, after you say your prayers, put your hands where it hurts. Talk to your sister [in prayer]. Get mad at her. Say whatever it is. Then, ask her to put her hands over your hands. Finally, ask the Lord to put his hands over both of your hands."

The patient wept. Her daughter with them in the examination room sobbed, and Suzette shed tears.

For some patients such as the woman angry at her deceased sister, Suzette suggests how they might pray at home. She lets them know that prayer does not have to be in a church building. They can pray in their bedroom, on the potty, or in the bath!

For other patients, she prays with them in the examination room. When a physical problem does not have a good explanation, she asks questions about what is going on in their life. Seeing that the patient is wearing a holy medal or a cross, Suzette might judge that prayer may be appropriate.

"I hold their hands and look in their eyes. I invite them to say a prayer, saying, 'Can we just say a quick prayer? Can we talk to God? Is that okay?'

"The patient might say, 'Yes, absolutely!' or 'Okay,' or be quiet. They may want me to pray for someone who has died. They may close their eyes.

"Most of those that I pray with already have an active church life. I'm just there to remind them.

"After saying a prayer, they talk about prayer and what else the patient might do to take care of themselves. The patient often adds, 'I was supposed to see doctor so-and-so, but because Jesus is speaking through you, I was meant to see you today.'

"When spending extra time [to pray] with one patient, I'll thank the next patient for waiting. 'The patient before you needed some extra time.' I joke and say, 'You can't kick a crying patient out. Thank you so much for waiting.'" Suzette charts in her notes that they prayed and what it was about. When they meet a year later for their annual appointment, the patient might offer a brief update.

Finally, Suzette prays not only with patients. She prays with her co-workers.

About four mornings a week, a handful of staff starts the day together with prayer. Before their office opens and the day begins, they gather for a few minutes. They use a prayer booklet that has a short scripture reading, a reflection, and a prayer. Because by group acclaim she reads quickly and with expression, Suzette leads the reading. They take a moment to add their own prayers.

"A medical assistant might pray for one of the doctors who had a difficult night. We might even go to his desk and say a short prayer! The Catholic kid in me thinks that I should sprinkle the doctor's desk with my holy water."

The morning prayer with co-workers started with only Suzette, a Catholic, and Gina, a non-Catholic, who had become close friends. While Gina comes from a family of faith used to praying aloud, it was a new practice for Suzette. She grew to like praying spontaneously and even becoming the prayer leader.

"When everyone present is Catholic, we'll pray the Lord's Prayer, the Hail Mary and the 'Glory be to the Father' doxology. It's nice, it's very nice."

In the course of the day, someone on staff might pull a co-worker aside for a short prayer as Suzette once did for her brother going to the Emergency Room. She had pulled Gina to the back of the office for a quick prayer for her brother. Where two or three are gathered in Christ's name, he is among them.

Praying with others has opened her up to more ways to pray. Suzette finds herself more at ease to pray in the moment. She prays with her teenage children at home. They won't pray aloud unless it is a familiar Catholic prayer, but they don't refuse when she puts her hands on them and prays.

"When I'm tired and want to go home and just be a mom, I can say, 'Lord, give me a patient who reminds me why I am here.' And it never fails. Someone affirms me, I have a good visit, and I close the door and look up to say, 'Okay God, that was good. Thanks.'"

Pray With Someone You Just Met

El Camino is a pilgrim route through Spain that ends in the medieval city of Santiago de Compostela. According to tradition, the bones of St. James the Apostle are buried in its Cathedral. For a thousand years, pilgrims have walked hundreds of miles to honor St. James and worship the Lord.

There are a number of Caminos or Ways to Santiago de Compostela. The most popular Camino is the French Way. Martin Sheen made a movie in 2010 about walking "The Way." The French Camino starts in France.

One week in June, my parents and I and three others were blessed to walk a week of the Camino. The route we walked was not the French Camino. It was the Portuguese Camino. The full Portuguese route starts in Lisbon, Portugal, and takes about five weeks to walk. We chose to walk the final week.

We started from Tui, a town on the Portugal-Spain border, and walked north to Santiago de Compostela in

Spain. The walk from Tui to Santiago was six days and averaged twenty kilometers per day. The walk was considered "moderate" but tested us in its length. The Tui-Santiago stage covered the final hundred kilometers of the route which was the minimum required to claim your Compostela certificate in Santiago.

The route took us through the region of Galicia in Northern Spain. We followed quiet country roads and woodland paths. We walked under canopies of grapevines leafing out on trellises and budding with their fruit. We felt drawn in by the gracious Galician pace where everyone except pilgrims took a siesta in the afternoon. Along the way, we prayed the rosary, visited with one another, and met other pilgrims. It was a walking retreat.

One morning we were able to give back a little in return for the kind hospitality we were shown. We were passing through a hamlet. The narrow road wide enough for only one car was lined by houses and apartments. Low walls separated our road from the patios. We could see flowers in every home. Some were purple foxgloves. Blue chrysanthemum blooms hung on bushes like Chinese lanterns. Some flowers were potted. Roses were planted along the wall. Some were climbing fragrant jasmine. No matter the simplicity of the home, they all were fragrant with flowers.

We stopped to smell the roses at one garden wall. It had a flowered archway over the gate. Like high school kids at the homecoming dance in front of the official photo spot, the six of us took pictures of each other in front of the gate.

As we turned to move on, one member of our group called us back. A handsome elderly woman, dressed in a gardening apron, had come out of the garden. With smiles and gesture she invited us through her flowered archway into her garden. "Vengan," she said. "Come."

She led us around a wooden garden shed into the rest of the garden. We saw bushes in formation, flowers in bloom. The woman reached up to a tree and pulled off some fruit. They were loquats, or in Spanish, nísperos. Our loquats in Florida were peach-colored oblong fruit about the size of a thumb and tasted rather bland. Her tree's fruit was more rounded and much more flavorful. We each tried the fruit, dropping the seeds into the garden at her invitation.

When I asked her where she lived, she pointed across the road to the apartment building. She added that this garden plot was hers. Rather than build a house on it, it was totally dedicated to being a garden. She went on to show us more flowers.

Pushing my conversational Spanish, I explained that we were pilgrims from the United States walking the Camino. She smiled, "Si, sí."

I pointed at the scallop shells framing a garden bed. "Usted tiene el símbolo del Camino, la concha." Her garden had scallop shells, the symbol of the Camino.

The pilgrims from centuries past pinned a scallop shell to their hat to show that they were pilgrims. Modern pilgrims hung the scallop shells on their backpacks or around their necks. The chapels along the way had the scallop shell design worked into arches and cornices. The shell designated the waymarks along the Camino.

The señora held up a hand. "Esperan," and went into her garden shed for a moment. She came back with a scallop shell for each of us. We had not had a shell of our own. Now we did. Receiving the symbol of the Camino made us feel that we truly were pilgrims on the Way.

I wanted to do something for her in return for her kindness. I said, "Soy sacerdote. Queremos orar para Usted. Que pide al Señor?" What do you want the Lord to do for you?

"No para mi," she pointed to the apartment building. "Para mi hija y para los enfermos del pueblo." She asked me to pray for her daughter and for the sick of the village. Her eyes became soft and teared up.

I prayed, "Por favor Señor, bendiga a esta señora. Bendiga a su hija. Cuida de los enfermos. Como ellos comparten en tu sufrimiento y cruz, puedan compartir en tu gloria y en la resurrección. Por Jesús Cristo nuestro Señor. Amen." As the sick share in the suffering and cross, I prayed, may they share in your glory and resurrection.

The señora embraced me and the rest of our little band. We went on our way with our camino shells and the kindness of the señora. Our day just begun was already blessed with prayer for one another!

PRAY IN THE EMERGENCY ROOM

Sometimes you take the initiative and ask, "Can I say a prayer with you?" And sometimes someone asks you if you can say a prayer. Rick Caldwell gave an example of a time he was asked to pray for someone. The example was part of a homily he gave in his training for the permanent diaconate.[6]

"I got a call the other day. I could hear the terror in my buddy's voice. His son had been in a car wreck and he needed me to come to the emergency room and pray with his family. I could hear the urgency in his voice and his great sorrow. I raced to the hospital.

"As I turned my engine off I said, 'God, I'm not sure what to say and what to do. Please give me strength.' I had taken on my friend's fear. I stopped in the restroom, locked the door, and got down on my knees. (Isn't it nice the hospital bathrooms are so clean?) Once again I said, 'God, I'm not sure what to do but give me the strength to be of some service.'"

Rick prayed not once but twice to God. He asked for God's help. Before he prayed with the friend and his family at the emergency room, he said his own prayer. He asked God for strength. He admitted he did not know what to say or do. After asking God for guidance, he got up from his knees and went to the emergency room.

"I went in the room where the family and the child were. The mom and dad were disoriented and silent. Like sheep without a shepherd, they were unprotected and lost. Their son was strapped to a gurney – tubes were in his arms, neck and throat – his life was being supported. Blood gurgled from his mouth as the oxygen inflated his lungs. Over the clean smell of the hospital room, there was almost a smell of death. Their other son knelt down beside the cold, stainless steel table."

Taking in the tragedy, Rick saw that the mother and father were in shock. Their son was near death. Another son knelt in prayer on the hard floor. Rick started to think as Jesus the Good Shepherd thought. He saw the family in need of guidance and protection. It was his turn to pray.

"As we prayed, the sun was setting brightly and peeked through the window. It was as if Jesus could see and could feel their pain."

Rick did not say in his homily what happened next. He did not tell us whether the son survived the car wreck or not. What he did tell us is that sometimes you do not know what to say when a friend asks you to pray. Speaking to God on behalf of someone in great need is an awesome responsibility. Like Rick, you might not feel up to the task.

What you can do is what Rick did. Lock the bathroom door. Get down on your knees. Ask God for the grace to say and do what he wants you to say and do.

Then get up from your knees and go to the person in need of prayer. You won't be going alone. The Lord Jesus will be praying with you. You'll be praying in his name "through Christ our Lord."

Your presence and prayer will bring the presence and power of Christ. Nothing less is necessary, nothing more could one offer. You will have done all that you could do and should do with the love of Christ.

Pray with Your Children

The first time that a person walked up to me after Mass and said, "Bendición," I did not know what to say. Bendición? I knew enough Spanish to know that the word "bendición" meant "blessing." But I was still learning about Spanish culture. What was he asking?

He was asking for a blessing.

Spanish cultures have a beautiful custom. A child comes before his mother or father and says, "Bendición." The parent places his hand on the child's head, or traces the sign of the cross on the child's forehead, and says, "Que Dios te bendiga." May God bless you.

Before going to school, children ask their parents, "Bendición." The parents bless them for protection and for help with their studies, "Que Dios te bendiga." May God bless you.

Before going out with friends, teenagers ask their parents, "Bendición." The parents bless them to be safe in the car and to return before curfew, "Que Dios te bendiga." May God bless you.

Aunts and uncles bless nephews and nieces, grandparents bless grandchildren, and godparents bless godchildren. Above all, parents bless children. "Que Dios te bendiga." May God bless you.

You would not let your children go to school without shoes. You are responsible for the physical well-being of your children.

You would not let your children out the door of your house without a hug and kiss. You care for them and want them to feel your care.

In the same way, you are responsible for their spiritual well-being. Why would you send your children into the world without a blessing?

You cannot always be with your children to protect them. You might worry about "stranger danger" or fear that your child will be bullied. What happens if during snack time she chokes on a peanut? Who will be there to help your child?

The good news is that you do not have to be with your children all of the time. The Lord is with them to protect them. The Lord is with them to help them.

When you give your blessing to your child, you receive peace of mind. You know and they know that the Lord is with them.

Giving a blessing is not just a custom from Spanish cultures. Giving your blessing is from Scripture.

In the Book of Numbers 6:22-27 the LORD said to Moses: "Speak to Aaron and his sons and tell them: This is how you shall bless the Israelites. Say to them:

The LORD bless you and keep you!

The LORD let his face shine upon you, and be gracious to you!

The LORD look upon you kindly and give you peace!

So shall they invoke my name upon the Israelites, and I will bless them."

You do not have to be Moses or Aaron or a Catholic priest to invoke a blessing. In virtue of baptism and confirmation, you have the ability to bless your children. You have the authority and responsibility to invoke the name of the Lord on their behalf.

If you do not already have the custom to bless your children, a good way to start this custom is at bedtime. You simply make the sign of the cross on the forehead of your child and say, "Que Dios te bendiga." May God bless you.

Your child may sleep better. Knowing that the Lord is watching over your child, you will sleep better.

You can pray with your children every day. As the Lord gives you children, he gives you the power to bless. As you have received, give. Give a daily blessing to your children and you will be blessed.

PRACTICAL TIPS FOR PRAYING WITH SOMEONE

Francis MacNutt, in his beautiful and inspiring book, *The Practice of Healing Prayer: A How-To Guide for Catholics*, offers some practical suggestions when you pray for the sick.[7] These suggestions apply as well to any prayer you might say with another person.

- Be specific. "May God bless you" sounds nice but can't hold a candle to "Lord, heal this person in body, soul, and spirit, and especially in their lower back. Take away the pain and restore it to full strength." When my back is sore, you can guess which prayer I want prayed over me.

- Do not say, "if it be your will." The key word is "if." Often the word "if" signals "I really don't think anything is going to happen and I want to give God (and me!) some cover when they are disappointed." This "if" goes back to the fear of looking foolish. It is true that all prayers depend on God's will. We cannot presume to tell God what to do. With confidence in God the Father, we submit to his will. His will, after all, is that we have abundant life (John 10:10). Your part is to pray with expectancy.

- Do say "thank you." Include a heartfelt thank-you to the Lord for hearing your prayer and answering it as he sees best. Gratitude is that attitude that nurtures faith.

- Touch appropriately. As you would gladly hug another person who is hurting, a simple touch of the hand on a safe place such as a shoulder or elbow connects you even more than words. Holding hands is a way to hold their hurting heart. Of course, ask before you touch. You can ask, "Is it okay if I put my hand on your shoulder while we pray?"

The other tip I would add from my own experience is to follow up the question, "Can I say a prayer with you?" with the question, "What do you want to pray for?" The question gave me an opening with Joe the contractor. Even though he gave me an "I'm not really interested" answer ("world peace"), it led to an experience of prayer that he found surprisingly meaningful.[8]

A few times the person has replied, "Nothing, I'm good." I simply said, "OK, maybe next time." We continued talking or doing whatever we were doing.

When I ask children, "What do you want to pray for?" they sometimes need prompting before deciding, "Family." Teenagers often reply, "School."

Whether the request is for family, health, children, grandpa, or the nation, it reveals what is on their heart. It takes the conversation to a deeper level. We are no longer just visiting. We are praying.

For Discussion

- "After Mass, people ask me to pray for a sick cousin in Puerto Rico, their family leaving on a trip, or perhaps for themselves going through a tough time." *Have you ever asked a priest to pray for you? If the priest prayed for you at that moment, what was it like?*

- "What might push us to take the risk and offer a prayer is a desperate situation. When someone you love is in a bad way, you may be ready to try anything. You may even dare to say, 'Let us say a prayer.'" *When have you dared to say, "Let us say a prayer"?*

Spiritual Exercise

Partner one-on-one with someone in your discussion group.

1. Ask them, "What do you want to pray for?"
2. Pray for your partner
    a. Be specific
    b. Do not say "if it be your will"
    c. Do say "thank you"
    d. Use touch appropriately
3. Then switch. Let your partner ask you, "What do you want to pray for?" and pray for you in turn.

TWO

SCRIPTURE SHOWS US HOW TO PRAY FOR OTHERS

The Scriptures show us how to pray for others. This chapter gives two examples from the Bible to help you put into action, "Can I say a prayer with you?"

The first example is the story how Abraham interceded for the city of Sodom. It shows that praying to the Lord for someone is like talking with a close friend on behalf of a common friend.

The second example from Scripture is the story how four men opened up the roof of a crowded house in order to lower a paralyzed man down to Jesus inside. His response was not what they expected – they received more than they asked for. The story shows how we are like the four men, lifting people up (or lowering them down!) to the Lord, and receiving more than we could hope.

ABRAHAM WAS A FRIEND OF GOD

Bishop Thomas Grady was the Bishop of Orlando when I was growing up. A tall man, he looked holy in his bishop robes.

Once after a Mass, a child asked Bishop Grady, "Are you Jesus?"

Bishop Grady replied, "No, but I'm a friend of Jesus."

Like Bishop Grady, Abraham was a friend of God. He walked and talked with God as friends do. He spoke directly about what was on his heart.

The first book of the Bible, the book of Genesis, tells us that the friendship between Abraham and the Lord began when Abraham was already an old man. Seventy-five years old, he heard a call from the Lord. The Lord told him uproot his wife Sarah, his nephew Lot, his servants, his flocks and tent, and move to a land of God's choosing.

Against common sense, Abraham did what the Lord told him to do. At an age when he was ready for retirement and content to spend the rest of his years with his aging wife, he struck out in faith as the Lord directed him. He moved everything a thousand miles from the Assyrian town of Haran to the land of Canaan. He left behind the safety of his ancestral homeland.

The big move was only the beginning of the Abraham's adventures with the Lord. The Lord promised Abraham at Shechem that he would give the Canaanite land to Abraham's descendants. The promise seemed empty when a famine drove Abraham and his family into Egypt. After a risky business between Pharaoh and Sarah and thanks to a protecting plague from the Lord, Abraham returned to Bethel. He put together a posse of three hundred men and battled four kings to rescue Lot and his household.

The move to Canaan, the famine, the migration to Egypt, the return to Canaan, and the battles along the way deepened Abraham's friendship with the Lord. What was decisive in their friendship though was when the Lord made a covenant with Abraham.

The Lord promised Abraham that his descendants would be as numerous as the stars of the sky. The Lord did not mean Abraham's physical descendants. He meant that countless spiritual descendants would share the same faith as Abraham. These spiritual children of Abraham would call him their father in faith and live in friendship with the Lord. Abraham's descendants in faith, the Lord promised, would be a blessing to the nations.[9]

Abraham for his part trusted God. He trusted the Lord even though he was old, had no children, and did not know where he was going. He trusted the Lord without the advantage that we have in knowing a bit more about the Lord's saving work.

Abraham's trust in the Lord was the basis of their friendship. Theirs was not a passing acquaintance. Theirs was a friendship based on trust.

ABRAHAM INTERCEDED WITH GOD FOR SODOM (GENESIS 18:16-33)

Abraham was a friend of God. In this context, let's look at how their friendship made a difference for others. This story is found in the first book of the Old Testament, the Book of Genesis.

One hot day while sitting at the entrance of his tent, Abraham looked up to see three men. Running to greet the desert travelers, he bowed low and begged them to rest for a while under the shade of the nearby oak of Mamre.

He had water brought to refresh their sore feet. He hurried into the tent and urged his wife Sarah to make bread for them. Meanwhile, he ran to his herd, picked out a choice calf, and had a servant prepare it. He himself brought curds and milk to the three visitors and waited on them while they took part in the spur-of-the-moment feast.

After they had eaten and before continuing on their way, the three visitors returned the hospitality of Abraham with a gift of their own. They promised that the old and childless Abraham and Sarah would bear a child within the year.

Sarah, hidden at the entrance of the tent, overheard the strange promise. She laughed to herself. Worn out and getting on in years, could she and Abraham still have pleasure together and bear a child?[10]

Walking with them from his tent, Abraham saw the refreshed visitors on their way to the city of Sodom. It is at this point that the Lord spoke to Abraham and revealed the purpose of the three visitors.

"The outcry against Sodom and Gomorrah is so great, and their sin so grave, that I must go down to see whether or not their actions are as bad as the cry against them that comes to me. I mean to find out."

The three visitors were divine messengers. Rather than bringing a message to Abraham, they were bringing a message to the Lord. They had been sent by the Lord to investigate the cry of the victims of injustice and violence in Sodom and Gomorrah.

The Lord would hear the suffering cry of the Hebrews enslaved under Pharaoh in Egypt (Exodus 3:7) and send Moses to set them free. He would hear the cry from the wronged widow and orphan and, turning the tables, make the wives of the oppressors into widows and their children into orphans (Exodus 22:21-23). He would hear the outcry against injustice and bloodshed and send prophets to pronounce his judgment upon those who acquitted the guilty for bribes and deprived the innocent of justice (Isaiah 5:7, 23).

The Lord heard the cry against Sodom. The visitors to Sodom aimed to discover what was happening in Sodom. Arriving in Sodom, they stayed at the home of Lot, the nephew of Abraham.[11]

Meanwhile Abraham, suspecting the doom of Sodom, could not stand silent before its destruction. Perhaps he worried for his nephew Lot and his family living in Sodom. He drew near to the Lord.

Abraham asked the Lord, "Will you really sweep away the righteous with the wicked? Suppose there were fifty righteous people in the city; would you really sweep away and not spare the place for the sake of the fifty righteous people within it?"

It was hardly just, Abraham reasoned, for the Lord to treat the righteous the same as the wicked and punish the good with the bad. It was unseemly for the judge of the world to do something so unjust.

The Lord considered Abraham's argument. "If I find fifty righteous people in the city of Sodom, I will spare the whole place for their sake."

Abraham had only begun to intercede. Acknowledging that he was only dust and ashes, he still dared to speak to the Lord. His reasoning would make any lawyer proud. "What if there are five less than fifty righteous people? Will you destroy the whole city because of those five?"

The Lord consented. What difference would five less than fifty righteous people make? If he found forty-five, he would spare the entire city.

Abraham persisted, saying, "What if only forty are found there?"

The Lord replied, "I will refrain from doing it for the sake of the forty."

Fearing the Lord's annoyance at his cheek, Abraham negotiated further. "What if only thirty are found there?"

The Lord replied, "I will refrain from doing it if I can find thirty there."

At this point, you would expect Abraham to back off. The first request to spare the city if fifty righteous people were found was bold enough. Three requests were the most one would expect. Yet for the fifth time, Abraham went on, "What if there are no more than twenty?"

"I will not destroy it," the Lord answered, "for the sake of the twenty."

Abraham threw caution to the wind and spoke up a sixth and final time. "What if ten are found there?"

"For the sake of the ten," he replied, "I will not destroy it."

Ten it was. The fate of Sodom hung upon ten righteous people. The Lord departed, and Abraham returned home.

In this story from the Book of Genesis, Abraham interceded for Sodom. Persisting on the behalf of the people of the city, he appealed to the Lord's sense of justice and honor and asked the Lord again and again for mercy upon the inhabitants of the city. His persistence went beyond polite conversation. Six times he asked the Lord for mercy. Six times the Lord consented to spare Sodom because Abraham asked.[12]

Abraham could plead with the Lord because he had walked with the Lord. Long before the day that three visitors came to his tent on their way to investigate the outcry in Sodom, Abraham and the Lord had a personal relationship.

Speaking freely and directly with the Lord was the fruit of his friendship with the Lord. He pleaded as friends do. Because of his pleas, the people of Sodom would live if there were only ten righteous people in the entire city.

Just as twelve was not a random number but signified the twelve tribes of Israel, ten was not a random number. Ten was the number of men needed to form a "minyan." A minyan was a quorum of ten men necessary for traditional Jewish public worship.

In other words, the survival of Sodom depended on the existence of a tiny faith community worshipping the Lord and living a righteous life. Worship and right living made the difference between life and death not only for the righteous, but for their neighbors and fellow citizens!

One thinks of the convents of cloistered nuns and monasteries of monks. They gather to pray five, six, or seven times a day. For three or more hours a day, they pray the psalms and scriptures together. What a difference they may well make in the well-being of their neighbors and fellow citizens.

A vibrant church, like ten righteous people in Sodom, can make such a difference to its community. The size does not matter. A small group of believers who worship the Lord and live their faith can protect and redeem even a people as wicked as Sodom.

The three visitors to Sodom, though, did not find ten righteous people. They did not find a faith community, however small, worshipping the Lord and living righteously. The fate of Sodom was sealed.

The three visitors urged Lot and his family to flee the city. At dawn the next day, the men now revealed as angels took Lot, his wife and two daughters by the hand. When they were led safely out of the city, fire and sulfur rained down upon Sodom and Gomorrah. The two cities and all of their inhabitants were destroyed.

The next morning, Abraham hurried to the place where he had interceded with the Lord on behalf of

Sodom. Looking down toward Sodom and Gomorrah and the whole region of the Plain, he saw smoke over the land rising like "the smoke from a kiln." All had perished for lack of a single worshipping community of faith.

Abraham's intercession with the Lord did not save the people of Sodom. Their fate depended on more than Abraham's prayer. In addition to his intercession, the faith and life of the people of Sodom mattered. As not even a small faith-filled community was to be found in Sodom, Abraham's prayer in itself was not enough to save the city.

His intercession though was not in vain. It did save Lot and his daughters. His pleading with the Lord had saved their lives.

The rest of Abraham's story is a lesson in hope. Abraham himself did not live to see the Lord's promises fulfilled. He did not live to see his sons and daughters in faith, as numerous as the stars in the sky, become a blessing to the nations.

Like Abraham, you might not see your prayer answered. Your prayer for others may likely depend on what others choose to do. Like Abraham, what you pray for may not even be realized in your lifetime. We do know that in the end Abraham's persistence with the Lord yielded fruit.

I hope that you know that Jesus calls you his friend. You can talk with him, walk with him, and even plead with him on behalf of others. I hope that you want nothing more in the world than to be like Abraham (and like Bishop Grady), a friend of Jesus.

THE CHURCH IS FOUR MEN ON THE ROOF (MARK 2:1-12)

The story of Abraham interceding with the Lord for Sodom shows us that praying for others can be like walking and talking with a close friend. A story from the New Testament about Jesus healing a paralytic shows that friends lifting a person up to the Lord – or lowering him down – can heal him, body and soul.

The last time he was in Capernaum, Jesus had taught the people as one having authority. He spoke the truth with power. Rebuking an unclean spirit in front of everyone in the synagogue, he commanded that the unclean spirit come out of a man. It did. All eyes were on Jesus.

After leaving the synagogue, Jesus healed the mother-in-law of Simon. That evening, as the crowd gathered at the door, he drove out demons and cured many who were ill. It had been an astounding end to a day such as no one had ever seen before.

Jesus slipped out of town early the next morning. Proving that it was no fluke, he preached in the synagogues of neighboring villages and cured the sick. He had even touched an untouchable leper and cured him.

When Jesus returned to Capernaum, everyone brought to Jesus their sick and suffering to be healed. No wonder the house in Capernaum was packed. So many crowded into the house that not one more person could come inside.

Suddenly, the roof opened. Sunlight bounced into the crowded room. Four guys on the roof widened a hole. They tore open the mud-and-sticks roof. While everyone watched, the four men lowered a paralyzed man on a mat. He came to rest in front of Jesus. No one said anything. Everyone waited to see what Jesus would say.

The four on the roof had made a gamble. The owner of the house would no doubt take notice that there was a man-sized hole in the roof of his house. Jesus might become upset that his teaching was interrupted. If Jesus did not appreciate the nerve of the four, the whole village would laugh.

Jesus was not upset. In fact, he was impressed by the faith of the four guys on the roof. The four guys on the roof were thinking not just outside the box. They were thinking outside the house! The four who carried the paralytic on the litter had found a way to bring their paralyzed friend to Jesus.

Jesus looked up at the four men on the roof. When he saw their faith, Jesus looked down at the paralytic and said, "Child, your sins are forgiven" (Mark 2:5). Instead of healing the man's body so that he could walk, Jesus healed the man's soul so that he could live.

Jesus Is the Divine Physician

I had had a surgical procedure on my right shoulder called a SLAP repair. The term SLAP stands for Superior Labrum Anterior and Posterior. The ring of cartilage that surrounded the socket of my right shoulder joint had a tear.

I wish I could say that the injury was from my major league pitching days with the Tampa Bay Rays. The cause of the injury was much more boring. Repetitive motion from swimming and gym exercises had torn the cartilage. (Note to self: listen to your body. If it hurts, don't do it!)

For months the pain in my right shoulder grew. Lifting the arm overhead hurt. Pain ran down my arm. Tucking in my shirttail with my right arm or reaching behind the passenger seat in the car became impossible. Favoring the right arm, I brushed my teeth with my left hand, made the sign of the cross with my left hand, and lifted up my arms to the Lord halfway.

For the initial treatment, my doctor prescribed anti-inflammatory drugs like ibuprofen and naproxen to reduce pain and swelling. He encouraged some exercises to restore movement and strengthen my shoulder. After some weeks of this treatment, the pain had not decreased. My range of motion was growing more limited.

An MRI showed that the problem was a cartilage tear. The specialist told me that cartilage does not heal itself. A torn muscle will heal in six to eight weeks. A broken bone will heal in ten weeks. Cartilage, though, does not heal.

If I wanted use of my arm, it needed surgery. The painful shoulder was becoming a frozen shoulder. The muscles were losing range of motion from lack of use. Even if I wanted to raise my right hand through the pain, I was losing the ability to do it.

The surgical procedure was rather simple. The surgeon cut three holes in my right shoulder. During the arthroscopic surgery, he put two anchors in the shoulder socket bone. He reattached the torn part with steel sutures held by the anchors. In less than thirty minutes, I was waking up in recovery.

The surgery was only the beginning of my healing. After several days with my arm in a sling, I began gentle exercises to increase the range of motion. Several weeks after the surgery, I began doing physical therapy. My physical therapist walked me every Wednesday afternoon through new exercises to loosen up my shoulder, pushing it to move a little further. I used stretchy bands to strengthen my shoulder muscles. Every day on my own, I repeated the exercises.

The experience was a painful lesson to listen to my body. It was expensive, too. Even though my health insurance was very good, I had to pay a couple thousand dollars out of pocket. I spent months in pain and slept poorly. I spent hours and hours doing exercises. It was not something I wanted to repeat.

Finally, after several months, I could tuck in my shirt-tail without pain. I could brush my teeth and comb my hair with my right arm. I could make the sign of the cross without pain.

I still could not pitch for the Tampa Bay Rays. No amount of physical therapy would get me onto a big league pitcher's mound. Thankfully, the care of the doctors and physical therapist and many others brought my arm to full motion and strength.

As wonderful as it is to be pain-free and healed in body, it's even more wonderful in the soul. Just as the body needs a doctor's care, so does the soul.

Sin can injure you in ways that you cannot heal yourself. No amount of time will make it get better. Praying in itself will not heal the wound. The pain persists. Just as my shoulder needed a doctor's care, a sin-sick soul needs a doctor's care.

The good news is that Jesus is the Divine Physician. In the gospel of Luke, the religious leaders wondered why Jesus ate with tax collectors. Jesus told them, "It is not the healthy who need a doctor, but the sick" (Luke 5:27-32).

Jesus came to take away the sins of the world. The physical healings he worked were visible signs of the more important spiritual healing. His greatest healing was from the cross. The first letter from Peter puts the mystery in this way, "By his wounds you have been healed" (1 Peter 2:24).

The Church is his hospital. The Church extends the healing ministry of Christ to heal the soul. The Church is not a hotel for saints. It is a hospital for sinners.

If the Church had a theme song for its healing ministry, it would be the African American spiritual, "There is a Balm in Gilead."

> There is a balm in Gilead
> To make the wounded whole;
> There is a balm in Gilead
> To heal the sin-sick soul.

A balm is a plant-based ointment with healing properties. The spiritual song recalls when the prophet Jeremiah pleaded for a balm in Gilead. He called on the power of God to save the people from their enemies (Jeremiah 8:22).

Forgiveness of sins is a great gift. Who wouldn't want their sins forgiven? But what about walking? In the story of the four men lowering the paralytic through the roof, Jesus had not given the four men what they came for.

The novelist Reynolds Price, wheelchair-bound with a large cancer on his spinal cord, wrote in his book *A Whole New Life* about a dream he had had. In the dream, Jesus led him into the water of the Sea of Galilee.

"Jesus silently took up handfuls of water and poured them over my head and back till water ran down my puckered scar. Then he spoke once – 'Your sins are forgiven' – and turned to shore again, done with me."

Reynolds Price wondered even as he dreamt, "But what about the cancer?"

Can God feed the countless souls who go to bed hungry every night? Can God quench the drug addict's craving, dry out the alcoholic, and lift the debt burdening the poor? Can God free the women caught in the despair and deceit of abortion?

With a paralyzed man dropped on his lap, Jesus transformed the interruption into a teaching moment.

Jesus knew that anyone could say, "Your sins are forgiven." To show that God was truly forgiving the man's sins, Jesus simply said to the paralytic, "Rise, pick up your mat, and go home." The paralytic rolled up his mat and went home.

The gamble of the four friends lowering the paralytic down to the Lord healed him, body and soul. The risk they took was well worth it.

Like the four guys on the roof, we lift up others to the Lord when we ask them, "Can I say a prayer with you?" We can even bring before the Lord a person who does not have faith!

How the Lord heals them is up to the Lord. Our part, through faith in the Divine Physician, is to bring others before the Lord. The Church is the four men on the roof. Thinking outside the box and praying together can heal others, body and soul.

OUR FATHER, WHO ART IN HEAVEN...

From the Scriptures we learn how to pray for one another.

Abraham walked and talked and pleaded with the Lord for the people of Sodom. Like Abraham, we learn that a close friendship with the Lord helps us to pray for another. We may not get the answer we want. But we have done our part.

The four men opened up the roof of a crowded house. They risked their reputation and Jesus' anger in order that Jesus might heal their paralyzed friend. Jesus, going beyond simply healing the man's paralysis, healed the man's sins. Like the four men on the roof, we can take risks to bring our cares before the Lord.

A third and final example from Scripture is from Jesus himself. When his disciples saw him praying, they asked him to teach them to pray. He taught them, "Our Father, who art in heaven...." (Luke 11:1-4).

Jesus teaches us that we can ask God for our heart's desire: please let your will be done, please give us today our daily bread, please forgive us our sins, please help us to forgive others, please save us from temptation, please protect us.

When you are in such shock over the fact that a person said yes to your mumbled "Can I say a prayer with you?", you might not know what to say next. Do you say a six-part prayer as Abraham did? Do you take a bold roof-opening leap of faith like the four men on the roof?

You can pray in these ways and more. Or you can simply pray with another person as Jesus taught his disciples to pray, "Our Father, who art in heaven, hallowed by thy name. . . ." And you'll be his disciple, too.

For Discussion

- "Jesus calls you his friend. You can talk with him, walk with him, and even plead with him on behalf of others. I hope that you want nothing more in the world than to be like Abraham (and like Bishop Grady), a friend of Jesus." *When was a time that you walked and talked with the Lord as with a friend? How was your prayer answered?*

- "The gamble of the four friends lowering the paralytic down to the Lord healed him, body and soul. The risk they took was well worth it. Like the four guys on the roof, we lift up others to the Lord when we ask them, 'Can I say a prayer with you?' " *When have you opened up a roof over the Lord with some friends? Did things happen as you expected?*

THREE

THE SAINTS SHOW US HOW TO PRAY FOR OTHERS

SOMETIMES IT IS HARD TO ASK FOR HELP

Once when I was visiting my sister and her family, I wanted to watch TV. My favorite baseball team, the Tampa Bay Rays, was playing my least favorite baseball team, the New York Yankees. It was a game that would determine whether the Rays would get into the play-offs. I had to watch the game.

My sister and her husband, not interested in America's pastime, were watching a TV show in another room. My brother-in-law kindly asked me if I wanted him to find the right TV channel for me. The television and cable system involved more than one remote control.

"No thanks," I said, "I can do it."

"You're sure?" he asked. "The TV is complicated."

I said, "I'm sure."

The TV had two remote controls. A third one was hidden in the couch. It took me ten minutes to figure out their dark magic and get the game on the TV, but in no way was I going to ask for help.[13]

You might also find it hard to ask for help.

Rather than wait for the kids to take out the kitchen trash, you hold your nose and do it yourself to get it done and avoid nagging. Often at work, it is faster to do it yourself and get it done the way you want it done.

If you are elderly and you can't open the jar, you don't open the jar and you go without. You don't get a ride to the store. You just don't go.

With more private matters, such as a marriage gone cold, kids out of control, or an addiction, it is really, really hard to ask for help.

SAINTS ARE PEOPLE WHO ASKED FOR HELP

Saints are people who asked for help. They did not let their pride get in the way. They are women and men who turned to the Lord in their need.

On January 8, 1894 in Zdunska-Wola, Poland, Raymond was born to a very holy Catholic family. His mother, Maria, and his father, Julius, were poor working class people who loved the Church and their family. They were both third order lay Franciscans and very devoted to raising their children in the Church.

Raymond was a wild young boy. His mother often worried about the direction of his life because of his constant mischief. One day, his exasperated mother cried at six-year-old Raymond, "I don't know what's going to become of you!"

Raymond ran from the house and down the dirt road to the village chapel. He knelt before the statue of the Blessed Mother. Many years later, he recounted, "I prayed very hard to Our Lady to tell me what would happen to me. She appeared, holding in her hands two crowns, one white, one red. She asked if I would like to have them – one was for purity, the other for martyrdom. I said, 'I choose both.' She smiled and disappeared."

After that day, Raymond changed. He was not the same. He became more calm and studious. He entered the seminary of the Conventual Franciscans in Lvív (then Poland, now Ukraine), where he took the name Maximilian Maria.

After ordination, Father Maximilian Kolbe founded a monastery at Niepokalanów near Warsaw that eventually grew to 800 Franciscan friars, the largest in the world at the time. He established a monastery in Japan and another in India. Promoting veneration of the Immaculate Virgin Mary, he founded a radio station and then a newspaper, which had hundreds of thousands of readers across Europe.

In 1941 during World War II, he was arrested by the German Gestapo and became prisoner #16670 at the Auschwitz-Berganau concentration camp.

When several prisoners escaped, the commandant selected ten prisoners to starve to death in a concrete basement cell called the Bunker. One of the doomed prisoners was Franciszek Gajowniczek. He cried out in despair, "Oh, my poor wife, my poor children. I shall never see them again."

It was then that the unexpected happened. From the ranks of those temporarily reprieved, prisoner #16670,

Father Maximilian Kolbe, stepped forward and offered himself in Gajowniczek's place. The surprised commandant consented to the exchange. The ten condemned men including Father Kolbe were led away to an underground cell. Stripped naked and given no food or water, they were doomed to die.

Bruno Borgowiec was an eyewitness of those last days. He was an assistant to the janitor and an interpreter in the underground Bunkers.

"In the cell of the poor wretches there were daily loud prayers, the rosary and singing, in which prisoners from neighboring cells also joined. When no SS men were in the Block, I went to the Bunker to talk to the men and comfort them. Fervent prayers and songs to the Holy Mother resounded in all the corridors of the Bunker. I had the impression I was in a church. Father Kolbe was leading and the prisoners responded in unison."

The prisoners begged for a piece of bread and a cup of water but received only a kick in the stomach by the SS men. They would be killed falling backward on the cement floor or shot to death.

"... Father Kolbe bore up bravely, he did not beg and did not complain but raised the spirits of the others.... Since they had grown very weak, prayers were now only whispered. At every inspection, when almost all the others were now lying on the floor, Father Kolbe was seen kneeling or standing in the centre as he looked cheerfully in the face of the SS men.

After two weeks, only Father Kolbe remained. The other prisoners had been killed or died. The authorities wanted the cell for new victims.

"So one day they brought in the head of the sick quarters, a German, a common criminal named Bock, who gave Father Kolbe an injection of carbolic acid in the vein of his left arm. Father Kolbe, with a prayer on his lips, himself gave his arm to the executioner."

Bruno Borgowiec returned to the cell immediately after the SS men and Bock had departed. He found Father Kolbe in a sitting position against the back wall. His eyes were open and his head had fallen sideways. His face was radiant and calm.

The date was August 14, 1941. As if guided by his devotion to the Immaculate Mary, he had died one day before the Solemnity of the Assumption of Mary.

Maximilian Kolbe was beatified by Pope Paul VI October 17, 1971. On October 10, 1982, Pope John Paul II declared Kolbe a martyr of charity. Franciszek Gajowniczek, the man whose place in the Bunker Kolbe had taken for himself, was present at Father Kolbe's canonization.[14]

Kolbe is to date the only saint who is venerated both as a martyr for the faith, represented by the red crown offered to him by the Blessed Mother in his childhood vision, and as a holy person, represented by the white crown.

St. Maximilian Kolbe is the patron saint of drug addicts, families, prisoners, journalists, and the pro-life movement.

All of these things took place after the young Raymond prayed to the Blessed Mother and asked for help.

Saints are people who asked for help. They knew that they could not handle life on their own. They needed help. They were not shy to ask the Lord in all things for his help. They surrendered their lives to him again and again. Asking for help opened up the way to heaven.

ASK THE SAINTS FOR HELP

When you ask a saint for their prayers, you will find an understanding ear. The saints, like friends in high places, gladly pray for you when you ask them for help. The saints know what it means to ask for help.

Now there are right ways and there are wrong ways to ask the saints for help.

Prowling for a parking space at the mall two days before Christmas, a man promised the Lord, "I'll go to church for Christmas, I'll give to the poor, I'll turn over a new leaf. Hail Mary full of grace, help me find a parking space!"

Just then a car pulled out of a parking space right in front of the main entrance. The man glanced upwards to heaven and said, "Never mind, Lord, I found a place to park."

That's the wrong way to ask for help. Saints are not on-call magicians to bail you out of jam.

Just as you develop a relationship with a friend who prays for you, you get to know the saints. A saint that you connect with in a special way is known as your patron saint.

In his book *My Life with the Saints*, Father James Martin relates how he came to know particular saints as guides and friends in high places.

For example, he studied French in high school, "taking dictation, doing drills, putting on playlets, giving speeches, and watching ancient filmstrips and movies about France and French culture."

One day the French teacher showed prized slides from his trips to France. One slide showed a statue of a young woman on a gleaming golden horse.

"Jeanne d'Arc," the teacher noted. Before anyone could ask who she was, the projector clicked to the next slide of a museum.

Some years later after college, James Martin took a trip through Europe. In Orleans, France, he recognized from that high school French class the statue of the woman on her horse.

The Baedeker guide told him that during the Hundred Years' War, the young peasant girl Joan heard the voices of three saints – St. Michael, St. Margaret, and St. Catherine – who instructed her to save France. Against all odds, Joan came to lead the army into battle in a suit of white armor and freed the besieged city of Orleans. In the religious and political twists of the age, she was later condemned as a heretic. Burned at the stake, her last words were, "Jesus, Jesus."

James Martin grew to admire this crazy young girl who heard voices, left her family, went to war, and was burned at the stake for an unseen person. Her witness gave him confidence in his own budding faith.

"Faith was something that seemed sensible and nonsensical at the same time." Inspired by the courage of St. Joan of Arc, James Martin began a journey of faith that eventually led him to the priesthood.

Father Martin writes how Therese of Lisieux is the person he thinks about when he feels dejected or discouraged. She understood the way that grace works through the petty struggles of everyday life.

When he has difficulties accepting a difficult decision from a superior, he turns to Ignatius of Loyola, who went from a soldier of fortune to the founder of the Jesuits. He turns to Pope John XXIII when struggling with the Church.

When he loses something, Father Martin remembers the prayer from childhood, "St. Anthony, St. Anthony, please come around. Something is lost and cannot be found." The car keys come out of their hiding place with amazing speed!

The saints, in short, are our friends. They have gone ahead of us and now cheer us along. The crowd watching a sport event gives the home team an advantage. Their cheering is like an extra man on the field. In the same way, "a huge crowd which no one could count from every nation, race, people, and tongue" surrounds us, rooting for us (Revelation 7:9).

The saints have an important role in the Easter Vigil. On this most holy night before Easter Sunday, the Church baptizes men and women into the death and resurrection of Christ.

During the Easter Vigil liturgy, we process to the baptism pool. The deacon leads the procession with the Paschal Candle, symbolizing Christ leading his people. As the deacon passes through the assembly, those to be baptized and their godparents leave their places in the pews and follow him. Like a conga line, the procession grows. The procession is accompanied by the Litany of the Saints. The assembly invokes the saints as it sings,

> Lord, have mercy. Lord, have mercy.
> Christ, have mercy. Christ, have mercy.
> Lord, have mercy. Lord, have mercy.
> Holy Mary, Mother of God, pray for us.
> Saint Michael, pray for us.
> Holy Angels of God, pray for us.
> Saint John the Baptist, pray for us.
> Saint Joseph, pray for us.
> Saint Peter and Saint Paul, pray for us.
> Saint Andrew, pray for us.

Saint John, pray for us.
Saint Mary Magdalene, pray for us.
Saint Stephen, pray for us.
Saint Ignatius of Antioch, pray for us.
Saint Lawrence, pray for us.
Saint Perpetua and Saint Felicity, pray for us.
Saint Agnes, pray for us.
Saint Gregory, pray for us.
Saint Augustine, pray for us.
Saint Athanasius, pray for us.
Saint Basil, pray for us.
Saint Martin, pray for us.
Saint Benedict, pray for us.
Saint Francis and Saint Dominic, pray for us.
Saint Francis Xavier, pray for us.
Saint John Vianney, pray for us.
Saint Catherine of Siena, pray for us.
Saint Teresa of Jesus, pray for us.
All holy men and women, Saints of God, pray for us.

We add to the Litany of the Saints the names of the patron saints of those to be baptized.

By the time the conga line arrives at the baptistery, there is a festive, expectant air. It is as if the saints have joined the conga line. Their presence and prayers support those about to be baptized into the death and resurrection of the Lord Jesus.

The saints are not invoked only during the Easter Vigil. When we baptize infants, we pray the Litany of the Saints. While there is not a conga line processing to the baptism font, the saints are present. Just as we ask family and friends to pray for the babies being baptized, we invoke the saints.

The Litany of the Saints is an important part of the liturgy for the ordination to the priesthood. As I lay face down on the floor of the Cathedral for my ordination to the priesthood, everyone sang the Litany of the Saints. I felt lifted up as if I were spiritually crowd-surfing and being passed hand-to-hand over the heads of the assembly and the saints, trusting that they would not drop me.

We chant the Litany of the Saints for the dying. Gathered with family and friends around the bed of the dying person, we are surrounded by the saints. What better way could there be to commend a person into the hands of the Lord. We invoke the saints to accompany the dying person on the same final journey that they themselves have made. The heavenly host fills the room.

We ask the saints for their help. In our liturgies and in our prayers, we turn to our friends in high places. After all, the saints were not shy to ask the Lord and his people for help. Even now, they are praying for you.

PADRE PIO OF PIETRELCINA

As suggested earlier, you might want to have a patron saint. A patron saint is a saint with whom you have a special connection. Your patron saint might be the saint you chose when you received the Sacrament of

Confirmation. It might be your baptism name. Padre Pio is such a saint with whom many people have had a special connection.

Francesco Forgione (Padre Pio) was born in the small farming town of Pietrelcina in southern Italy on May 25, 1887. He became a Capuchin monk in the Italian monastery of San Giovanni Rotondo. He was ordained a priest in 1910. He loved to pray the rosary. Pilgrims came from around the world to attend his Mass and make their confession.

Padre Pio is credited with the healing of many people. He founded a hospital called Casa Sollievo della Sofferenza (House for the Relief of Suffering) that opened in 1956. He founded prayer groups that have spread worldwide and pray for the Church's suffering Body.

Ironically, he himself suffered lifelong from severe headaches, dizziness, asthma, intestinal trouble, chest pains, pulmonary infections, back pain, bronchitis, fevers, and more.

These pains and illnesses were minor compared to the pain from the stigmata. Eight years after ordination, while saying his prayers of thanksgiving after Mass, Padre Pio received the wounds of Christ's crucifixion in his hands, feet and side. The first priest in the history of the Church to receive the wounds of Christ, he bore them without complaint for fifty years.[15]

The slightest touch to his hands caused acute pain. He walked in a shuffle and stood on the edges of his feet and heels so as not to press on the wounds of his feet.

Jesus healed many who suffered. He gave sight to the blind, made the mute speak, and cast out demons. The one person that Jesus never helped with his power was himself. He never worked a miracle, such as change stones into bread to eat when he was fasting in the desert, which would have benefitted his own self. His life and death were completely given for others.

Padre Pio, like Jesus, healed many who suffered. Like Jesus, he did not benefit from his spiritual gifts of healing. He suffered the scourging, crown of thorns and the shoulder wound of Christ too excruciating to be described. In his hands, feet, and side, he bore the sufferings of Christ for the salvation of many. Pope Paul VI summed up his person, saying, "He was a man of prayer and suffering."

Many of the pilgrims have given testimonies about the intercessions of Padre Pio. A sampling of their stories gives witness to what can happen when you ask a saint to pray for you:

Father Alberto D'Apolito was a fellow monk who asked Padre Pio to pray for Maria Pia. She had been admitted to the hospital with a serious condition. Her father Gino wanted to know if he should take his daughter back home to Biella.

"She should not be moved from the hospital," Padre Pio replied. "If she needs an operation, she should be operated on here and not in Biella."

Father Alberto responded that Gino was a poor man. He could not afford the hospital or the operation. Could Padre Pia invoke a cure from the Blessed Virgin for Maria Pia so that she would not require an operation?

"Yes, I will pray about it," Padre Pio answered.

When Dr. Gusso, the head physician of the Home for the Relief of Suffering, examined Maria Pia several hours later, he found that she was completely well. She was sent home. Her miraculous recovery took place on September 22, 1968, one day before Padre Pio's death.[16]

Kevin Hale, on his twenty-first birthday, attended Padre Pio's Mass. After the Mass, he brought a crucifix to Padre Pio, who kissed it and blessed it. He could smell a fragrance of cinnamon and roses that lasted nearly an hour.

While saying his night prayers, he asked his guardian angel to go to Padre Pio and tell him of all his spiritual needs. The following night Kevin gathered with the villagers in the plaza below Padre Pio's cell to bid goodnight to Padre Pio. He came to the window and gave everyone his blessing and spoke to the group in Italian.

When Kevin asked the woman next to him who spoke English what Padre Pio had said, she told him that Padre Pio said that he had been kept awake the previous night by a guardian angel from America.[17]

Even though decades have passed since his death in 1968, over seven million pilgrims come to his tomb each year, second in annual visitors only to the shrine of Our Lady of Guadalupe, Mexico.

Padre Pio had often declared, "After my death I will do more. My real mission will begin after my death." Since his death, testimonies to the intercession of Padre Pio abound. Here are a few.[18]

"After suffering for ten years, in December, 1983, I started the novena to Padre Pio. In February, my condition grew worse. My ankles became swollen and the pain was unbearable. On February 10th, I was healed in a dream."

Gregory William Collins dreamed that he was in a beautiful chapel. Padre Pio, coming to him, touched his swollen ankles and his back, saying, "Get up and walk. You are healed."

"I awoke immediately from my bed and I walked without a single pain in my body. That morning I attended Mass to thank our Lord. The pain came back, but only for a moment because soon what felt like a warm hand touched my back and took my pain away. I have never known that pain again."

Pasquale Presta wrote that she had been in a dark and frightening mental state. After her mother told her about

Padre Pio, she began to pray daily asking Padre Pio for his intercession.

"Then one night, I awoke suddenly and saw the figure of a monk in a brown robe with a beard. The next morning I told my mother of this experience. She told me it was Padre Pio watching over me. From that night onward I began to feel better. Today I feel great and I am a dedicated follower of Padre Pio."

"My daughter Elizabeth was 8 years old when she was diagnosed with Hodgkins disease, a type of cancer. She stayed at Our Lady's Children's Hospital in Dublin for a number of weeks."

One day, the head nurse who was a nun took aside Elizabeth's father, Michael Gormley. She broke the news that his daughter Elizabeth was dying from the cancer. He went to see Father John at the Capuchin Friary in Dublin. At his request, Father John went to the hospital and blessed Elizabeth and all the children in the ward with a glove from Padre Pio.

"Not long after, I was having a meal at the Fish and Chips restaurant on Kimmage Road in Dublin. Suddenly, the whole area was pervaded with the fragrance of roses. I instantly knew it was Padre Pio. I also thought to myself that it was an odd place for him to make his presence known. A few days later, I spoke to the head nurse again. She told me that she had astounding news for me – all of Elizabeth's tests were normal."

The daughter recovered completely thanks to the intercession of Padre Pio. She went on to sing professionally throughout Europe.

The Church does not make saints. God alone is holy and only God can make someone holy. The Church though officially recognizes a holy person. Part of the canonization process is a miracle attributed to the deceased person.

Padre Pio was canonized a saint on June 16, 2002. The miracle attributed to Padre Pio was the cure of a little boy, Matteo Colella, in January 2000.[19]

Matteo, age 7, took ill with a fever that rapidly worsened into skin hemorrhage and pulmonary edema. He was moved to the intensive care unit and put into a drug-induced coma. During the ten days of his coma, his mother prayed. Many others joined her prayers for her son.

Having a devotion to Padre Pio, she was able to pray the rosary at the tomb of Padre Pio. "While praying with my face pressed against the cold granite, I see with my eyes closed, in black and white, a bearded friar decisively approach a bed, and with both his hands he lifts all at once the rigid little body of a child to put him on his feet. It lasts only an instant! I open and re-close my eyes in the hope of seeing this scene continue. But my mind can no longer succeed in producing images, I am in darkness and my heart in the meantime begins to pound strongly.

I realize that the friar is Padre, and that perhaps while I am there, over the place of his remains, abandoned in my sorrows as a mother, so very close to him, he wishes to tell me: 'I will help Matteo to rise.' This I believe, I believe it strongly, I accuse myself of being irrational, but this I believe and I repeat: 'Jesus, I trust in you against all hope.'"

At another point in her 10-day vigil, she was enveloped in a pleasing and penetrating perfume. Several other events convinced her that Padre Pio was in heaven praying for her son on earth.

When Matteo finally awoke, she asked him what he remembered.

" 'Yes, I saw myself!'

" 'How did you see yourself?' I ask him curiously.

" 'I saw myself while asleep, from a distance, all alone in that bed,' Teo told me.

" 'Oh!' I replied. 'My poor love was all alone. And there were no doctors, nurses, mamma or papa?'

" 'No,' adds Teo.

"Then he closes his eyes again. Evidently he is concentrating on his memories. He reopens them suddenly and adds: 'No, mamma, I was not alone!'

" 'And who was with you?' I ask him.

" 'There was an old man, old with a white beard,' he replies.

"At that moment I do not understand and ask, perplexed: 'And how was this man dressed?'

" 'He had on a long, maroon garment.'

" 'And what was he doing?' I ask.

" 'He gave me his right hand and said to me, "Matteo, don't worry, you will get better soon." '

Matteo's mother's heart began to beat like crazy. She thought that she knew who Matteo had seen, but she wanted to be sure. She gave Matteo a little image of Padre Pio and waited for his reaction.

"He looked attentively at it for a little while, with his eyes all bright and with an unexpected joy, then he said to me with his lips, 'It is him, mamma, it is him, it is Padre Pio. It was Padre Pio who was with me!' "

CAN THE SAINTS SAY A PRAYER WITH YOU?

A girl drawing intently was asked by her mother, "What are you drawing?"

She replied, "I'm drawing God."

Her mother said, "No one knows what God looks like."

The girl busy with her crayons did not bother to look up. "They'll know when I'm finished."

We look at saints to see beautiful drawings of God. The saints are models of faith. They show us how to live as Christ. They show us his amazing love for us.

We do not worship saints. We worship God alone. We honor the saints even as they worship the Lord God.

Patron saints like Padre Pio are a gift from the Lord. They put a human face on the help that the Lord wants to give us.

For the teenager wondering what he will become when he grows up, consider getting to know St. Aloysius Gonzaga, patron of Christian youth.

If you suffer from headaches, you have a friend in St. Teresa of Avila, patron saint of headache sufferers.

Physicians can turn to St. Luke, police officers to Michael the Archangel, and Bible scholars to St. Jerome.

What do you do if you don't have a patron saint? How do you develop a devotion to a friend in high places?

Do what the saints do. Ask for help. Ask the Lord for a special saint, someone you can turn to, who can look out for you. Set aside your pride and ask for help.

If you can't do it for yourself, do it for the person you want to pray for. Ask a saint to pray for both of you as you offer a prayer.

Jesus taught that where two or three are gathered in his name, he is among them. You can invite a saint into your little gathering as you say, "Can I say a prayer with you?"

Saint Maximilian Kolbe, pray for us.
Saint Joan of Arc, pray for us.
Saint Ignatius of Loyola, pray for us.
Saint Therese of Lisieux, pray for us.
Saint Anthony of Padua, pray for us.
Saint Padre Pio, pray for us.

For Discussion

- "You might also find it hard to ask for help. . . . Rather than wait for the kids to take out the kitchen trash, you hold your nose and do it yourself to get it done and avoid nagging. At work, it is faster to do it yourself and get it done the way you want it done." *When did you ask for help? What happened?*

- Father James Martin writes how Therese of Lisieux is the person he thinks about when he feels dejected or discouraged. When he has difficulties accepting a difficult decision from a superior, he turns to Ignatius of Loyola, who went from a soldier of fortune to the founder of the Jesuits. He turns to Pope John XXIII when struggling with the Church. When he loses something, Father Martin remembers the prayer from childhood, "St. Anthony, St. Anthony, please come around. Something is lost and cannot be found." *What saint do you have a special connection with? When did you ask him or her for help? What happened?*

- "Padre Pio, like Jesus, healed many who suffered. Like Jesus, he did not benefit from his spiritual gifts of healing. In his hands, feet, and side, he bore the sufferings of Christ for the salvation of many. Pope Paul VI summed up his person, saying, 'He was a man of prayer and suffering.'" *How do you reconcile the fact that Padre Pio healed many yet greatly suffered?*

Spiritual Exercise

- "Jesus taught that where two or three are gathered in his name, he is among them. You can invite a saint into your little gathering as you say, 'Can I say a prayer with you?'" *Take a moment to ask a saint to pray with you for someone else. Remember to thank them!*

FOUR

How Do You Ask Someone to Pray for You?

The Pope Can Ask For Prayers

Pope Francis, during his September 2015 apostolic visit to the United States, met with the schoolchildren of Our Lady Queen of Angels School in East Harlem, New York.[20] People crowded along the street to see him. In the midst of the caravan of a half-dozen big black SUVs blinking red and blue lights followed by an even bigger brown SWAT van, Pope Francis waved and smiled from the side window of a tiny black Fiat. The children waved yellow flags and chanted, "Holy Father, we love you!"

He met with a smaller group in a classroom. When the children sang in English and in Spanish, "Make me a channel of your peace . . ." from the song, "The Prayer of Saint Francis," Pope Francis gestured for them to sing louder. Everyone laughed.

They prayed together. With hands in prayer, the Pope and the children prayed, "Hail Mary, full of grace. . . ." A boy showed him photos from their First Communion. A girl guided his hand to use a touch screen.

The Pope spoke to them in Spanish.[21] He told them that he was very happy to be with them. He thanked the teachers for letting him visit and steal a few minutes of their class time.

"How nice it is to feel that our school, or the places where we gather, are a second home." Noting that many of the students were from other countries, he added,

"This is not only important for you, but also for your families. School then ends up being one big family. A family where, together with our mothers and fathers, our grandparents, our teachers and friends, we learn to help one another, to share our good qualities, to give the best of ourselves, to work as a team, for that is very important, and to pursue our dreams."

He encouraged the children to dream like Reverend Martin Luther King, Jr., who dreamed that everyone would have opportunities and education. He encouraged the parents and teachers to dream that the children would grow up and be happy, bringing joy to everyone.

"All of you here, children and adults, have a right to dream and I am very happy that here in school, in your friends and your teachers, in all who are here to help, you can find the support you need. Wherever there are dreams, wherever there is joy, Jesus is always present…. Because Jesus is joy, and he wants to help us to feel that joy every day of our lives."

His final remarks before leaving were to give them homework.

"Before going, I would like to give you some homework." He spoke, "homework," in English to make sure that everyone understood. He laughed along with everyone else. "Puedo hacer? Can I?"

The crowded room roared, "Sí!"

"It is just a little request, but a very important one. Please don't forget to pray for me, so that I can share with many people the joy of Jesus."

Pope Francis added that he was not the only person in need of prayer. "And let us also pray that many other people can share joy like your own, whenever you feel supported, helped and counseled, even when there are problems. Even then, we still feel peace in our hearts, because Jesus never abandons us."

He gave them his blessing, "May God bless everyone of you today and may Our Lady watch over all of you."

The Pope had asked for their prayers. The most famous man on the planet had asked a classroom of children to pray for him. Everyone had expected him to pray for the children. That was what the pope did. But he made it clear that even the pope needs prayers, and he was not too important that he could not ask for prayers.

What Pope Francis was doing was nothing new. Saint Paul regularly requested prayers to support his ministry.

"Persevere in prayer, being watchful in it with thanksgiving," Paul wrote to the congregation in Colossae east of Ephesus. Writing the Letter to the Colossians from prison, he asked for their prayers. "At the same time, pray for us, too, that God may open a door to us for the word, to speak of the mystery of Christ, for which I am in prison" (Colossians 4:2-3). Paul asked them to pray not that he would escape suffering, but that the preaching of Christ would continue.

Paul asked the church in Thessalonica to pray similarly for the mission to preach Christ. "Finally, brothers, pray for us, so that the word of the Lord may speed forward and be glorified, as it did among you." In this letter, he put in a request for his own well-being, asking, "that we may be delivered from perverse and wicked people, for not all have faith. (2 Thessalonians 3:1-2).

"With all prayer and supplication, pray at every opportunity in the Spirit." The exhortation to pray constantly concluded Paul's letter to the Ephesians. It was a final parting word that Paul wanted them to remember above all. It was his marching orders to them. Paul added a request for prayers for his own ministry ". . . to make known with boldness the mystery of the gospel for which I am an ambassador in chains, so that I may have the courage to speak as I must" (Ephesians 6:18-20).

Pope Francis, as a successor to the apostles and especially to Peter the Apostle, was following in the footsteps of the apostles. I have no doubt that Peter and Paul would have made the same prayer request to the school children of Our Lady Queen of Angels School in East Harlem, New York.

The "homework" assignment by Pope Francis to the school children was not the first time that Pope Francis had made a public request for prayers. He had asked for prayers from the first moment that he was pope.

On March 13, 2013, under a rainy dark night, the crowds exploded in St. Peter's Square. Trumpets rang out and drums thumped as the 76-year old Argentinian Cardinal Jorge Mario Bergoglio was introduced on the balcony as the new pope.[22]

Asking for their prayers for his retired predecessor Pope Benedict XVI, the new Pope Francis led the hundreds of thousands of the faithful to pray, "Our Father, who art in heaven . . ." and "Hail Mary, full of grace, . . ." He finished with the doxology, "Glory be to the Father, to the Son, and to the Holy Spirit. . . ." He encouraged them to pray for one another and for the whole world.

Before he gave his first blessing to his flock as the new Bishop of Rome, Pope Francis said, "First I ask a favor of you: before the Bishop blesses his people, I ask you to pray to the Lord that he will bless me." He bowed from the waist in silent prayer while the faithful below bowed their heads and prayed for him. There was a holy silence in the great plaza of St. Peter.

Then Pope Francis raised his hand and gave his blessing to the people. He prayed for them, "May the blessing of Almighty God, the Father, the Son and the Holy Spirit, descend upon you and remain with you always."

Even as the new Pope Francis took his leave for the night, he asked the people again for their prayers. "Brothers and sisters, I leave you now. Thank you for your welcome. Pray for me and until we meet again . . . . Good night and sleep well!"

Pope Francis, on that rainy night of his election to the papacy, not only asked the people to pray for him. He took the time to let them pray for him. He bowed his head in silence while the people prayed for him.

When it was his turn, he blessed the people. He did not say, "I will pray for you during my prayers tonight," or "I will say a blessing for you later on." He took the time to bless them there and then.

Praying for someone and asking for their prayers is in real time. It need not be given as a rain check to fulfill later. You can ask for a prayer and bow your head to receive the prayer. If it is good enough for Pope Francis, it is good enough for us!

CLERGY CAN ASK FOR PRAYERS

In addition to serving various churches through ordained ministry, Richard and his wife had raised six children. He had been a minister for many years. He had a deep prayer life with the Lord. Yet Richard found himself again and again at his wits' end. His youngest son, a teenager, struggled with mental illness.

In the midst of their trials, the prayers of strangers gave him hope.

One day, Richard had to call the police. His son had become violent. The police handled the situation gracefully so much so that his son peacefully walked with the police out the front door of their home into the police car. He was wearing handcuffs as a precaution.

At that exact moment, Richard's next door neighbor drove up. Richard had met his neighbor only once before when a ball went into his neighbor's backyard. They had exchanged pleasantries and Richard got his ball back.

Richard did not know what his neighbor would make of the spectacle of his son with the police.

The neighbor, rather than close his garage door and mind his own business, walked over to Richard's house. They talked. The neighbor turned out to be a Baptist missionary. At one point, the neighbor said, "Can I pray for you?" Separated by denomination, united in prayer, the Baptist missionary prayed for the Methodist minister.

On another occasion, Richard had taken his son to an inpatient behavioral center to be involuntarily committed. Overcome with sadness, Richard went outside. He sat down on a low wall and cried.

A small black woman came along carrying a Bible. She walked up to him, an aging white man who was sobbing his eyes out. She started to pray for him and she did not pray quietly. She prayed loudly and for all to hear. The black Pentecostal woman prayed for the white Methodist minister, "In the name of Jesus!"

It was not the way prayer usually went. Normally, the minister prayed for the person. In this case, a passerby who happened to work at the behavioral center prayed for the minister. Their prayers and tears did not end the sufferings of Richard's son. The son was not dramatically healed. But Richard the ordained minister knew beyond a doubt that he needed people such as the Pentecostal woman and the Baptist neighbor to pray with him and for him so that he could in turn minister to others in the name of Jesus.

I myself have learned not to be shy about asking for prayers.

We were getting ready for the Easter Vigil when a call came to visit someone at the hospital.

"Really?" I thought. "Do they really need to see a priest right now?"

The Easter Vigil was a three hour liturgy. It started with the lighting of the Easter fire and the Paschal candle. There were special readings from Scripture, seven in all, for the Liturgy of the Word. We would be soon baptizing eight people. It was the mother of all vigils.

I wanted to be preparing myself in prayer. I was giving final thought to my homily. Going to the hospital was not on my last-minute list for the Easter Vigil. The hospital was across town. I calculated that if I went right away, I just might make it back in time.

As I jumped in my car, I made a little prayer, "Lord, I'll take care of this hospital visit if you'll take care of the Easter Vigil."

Naturally, every traffic light along the way turned red as if they were waiting especially for me. My anxiety shot up. Stuck at yet another red light, I made a phone call to the first person I could think of who might not be busy with the Easter Vigil.

Lothar picked up the call. "Hallo?" Lothar was German.

I had known Lothar and Leisha for fifteen years. We had first become friends when I was the parochial vicar at another church, Saints Peter and Paul. As fate would have it, they bought a house in the parish where I would eventually be appointed pastor. Small world!

"Lothar, it's David. I need a favor."

"Sure. What do you need?"

"I'm on my way to the hospital to visit someone. I need to get back to the parish in time for the Easter Vigil. Can you say a prayer for me?"

I heard what I had hoped. "Okay, we'll pray for you right away."

"And please pray for the person I'm visiting."

Lothar hung up. I found out later that he and Leisha said a prayer for me right away. They were foster parents for four young children. The children prayed too.

At the moment, all I knew is that the red light turned green. All of the traffic lights turned green. I felt like I was a one-car presidential motorcade. Traffic stopped for me as I drove no higher than the speed limit yet crossed town in record time.

I found a parking spot at the hospital without any problem. The patient was in her room and extremely grateful for my visit. We prayed. I anointed her. We talked for over a half hour.

The road back to the parish was as magical as the road to the hospital. The green lights stayed green as if on command. The route to the hospital and back had never been so swift. I arrived refreshed and not at all stressed as I had feared. There was plenty of time to get ready for the Easter Vigil.

Asking Lothar and Leisha to pray for my hospital visit made a difference. It took away my anxiety. Their prayers let me truly minister to the patient in the hospital. It prepared me spiritually to celebrate the Easter Vigil better than I could have prepared if I had remained in the parish and not visited the hospital.

Being a priest, I am not always comfortable asking for prayers. After all, my position by definition is to pray for others. Sometimes it is hard to turn it around and ask for prayers. Remembering that Easter Vigil helps me ask for prayers. Prayer works!

CAN YOU ASK FOR PRAYERS?

I asked through Facebook for stories when someone said a prayer on the spot. The responses showed that my experience was not a fluke. Ordinary people can have a wonderful experience from someone praying over them. Here are a few.[23]

Annie Bridges was on her way to see her mother before she died. The woman behind the airline counter questioned why Annie had changed her flight from Friday to Thursday. In November 2001, only two months after 9/11, security was tight.

"When I told her my mom was getting ready to pass, she stood up on the suitcase platform and asked everyone to stop and bow their heads and pray for my mother. Everyone stopped. She asked Jesus to be with my family and me during that time. Here we were at the counter and all of the people in line were praying for me, my mother and family."

The prayer lifted up Annie for the next six hours until she was with her family. Although her mother died before she arrived, Annie was comforted by the prayer. On the phone that morning, her mother had told her "she would love me forever."

Dianne (Turner) Kelter is a retired Police chaplain for the Lakeland Police Department. One afternoon she was called to the hospital. A six year old boy riding his bike had been run over by a van. Tire marks were on his shorts.

"When I got there the little boy was having a MRI to check for his injuries. I sat with the little boy's [Hindi] mother and through a translator I asked if she would teach me a prayer in Hindu. She did. After we prayed her prayer she asked me through a translator to teach her one of my prayers, so I taught her the Our Father and we prayed it."

Shortly after they finished praying, the doctor came. Fully expecting injuries, he could not explain the fact that the boy had no injuries.

"We both smiled and I left the hospital thanking God for hearing the prayers of two mothers."

Chris Monteleone visited Peter weekly at an assisted living facility. Before she had hip replacement surgery, she went to see him. Peter, soon turning one hundred years old, asked if he could pray for her.

"He stood over me and held my hands as he asked for blessings for me and the surgical team. He asked God to heal me quickly and completely. His words were spontaneous and heartfelt. When he finished he hugged me and asked me to let him know how everything went."

Her surgery and recovery went so smoothly that in three weeks she was able to visit Peter. She was convinced that his prayers, along with the prayers of friends and family, gave her the peace that everything would be okay. And it was!

Nancy Rivera-Heyboer recalled when she was a student attending the Franciscan University of Steubenville she suffered so much pain in her back that she could hardly walk. She had dropped from a full-time to a part-time student.

"One night, I went to a charismatic prayer service at the university. There were groups of people that would pray for you if you wanted. I went up to this one group that consisted of one deacon, one nun, and two other students. The nun asked me what did I need prayers for. I told her that my back pain is pretty bad and that in the past I had many pray over me but nothing happened, but that I wanted to stay at this university and needed my back to get better."

The nun and the others, laying hands on Nancy, prayed for her in English and in tongues. Although her back pain was still present, she felt great. She returned to her seat to pray.

"As I was praying and thanking God for this gift, I felt him tell me this in my soul, 'You are ungrateful.' So I apologized to God and said that I am grateful for all he has given me and if I was to continue with pain for Him to give me the grace to deal with it."

At that moment, the nun tapped her on the shoulder. "I don't know if this means anything to you, but as I prayed for you and after you left, I felt the Lord telling me one word in reference to you."

Nancy asked what the word was.

"Ungrateful."

Nancy said that the Lord had said as much to her. The nun replied, "Then the Lord has confirmed it to you."

From that experience of prayer with others, Nancy knew that the Lord was with her in good times and in bad. She was never alone even if she felt alone. The grew in her own prayer and in perseverance.

The Pope can ask for prayers. Ministers and priests can ask for prayers. Countless people can ask for prayers. Why not you?

You can ask for prayers. Just as you can ask someone if you can pray with them, you can ask them to pray with you. When you let someone pray with you, the grace of God's presence and power is with you right then and there.

I look forward to the next time I ask through Facebook for stories about prayer. May many more stories be told of God's goodness.

All it takes is a spark. The next time you would like strength, reach out and ask, "Can you say a prayer for me?"

For Discussion

- "Lothar hung up. I found out later that he and Leisha said a prayer for me right away. They were foster parents for four young children. The children prayed too. At the moment, all I knew is that the red light turned green. All of the traffic lights turned green. I felt like I was a one-car presidential motorcade. Traffic stopped for me as I drove no higher than the speed limit yet crossed town in record time." *Have you seen the fruits of someone's prayer for you?*

- "When I told her my mom was getting ready to pass, she stood up on the suitcase platform and asked everyone to stop and bow their heads and pray for my mother. Everyone stopped." *Has someone prayed for you in public? What happened?*

- "As I was praying and thanking God for this gift, I felt him tell me this in my soul, 'You are ungrateful.' So I apologized to God and said that I am grateful for all he has given me and if I was to continue with pain for Him to give me the grace to deal with it." *Prayer by others can heal more than the body. It can heal the soul. Have you had this experience?*

FIVE

WHAT CAN YOU SAY ABOUT SUFFERING?

"Can I say a prayer with you?" is a Christian response to someone as they open up about a child who has lost his way, a cancer in the family, or a desperate search for a job. The question, "Can I say a prayer with you?" not only shows you care. Your question shows that you are doing something about it. You are lifting them up to the Lord.

But what about suffering? Why is there suffering at all? Why do bad things happen to good people? Why does God permit evil? What is God doing about suffering?

When you pray with someone who is suffering, they may need to talk about the meaning of their suffering. This chapter helps you consider what you might say to someone about their sufferings.

WITH FRIENDS LIKE THESE, WHO NEEDS ENEMIES?

The story of Job in the Old Testament grapples with suffering. Job, you may recall, was a God-fearing man whose faith was pushed to the limit. In one horrible day, messenger after messenger brought him bad news and more bad news.

The first messenger ran up to tell him that raiders had carried off his donkeys and oxen and put to the sword his servants. The messenger had not finished before the next messenger arrived to tell Job that fire from heaven struck and consumed his sheep and shepherds. He was interrupted by a messenger who reported that Chaldeans rustled his camels and slaughtered more servants. The final messenger brought the tragic news that a great wind had collapsed his house upon a dinner party and killed all of his sons and daughters.

As if his misery was not complete, Job was stricken with severe boils from the soles of his feet to the crown of his head (Job 1-2). He had lost his wealth, his children, and his health.

Three friends sat with Job in silence for seven days and seven nights. When they finally spoke, their words were hardly a comfort.

Eliphaz the Temanite explained that God's ways are mysterious. We are nothing before God's greatness. Who are we to question God's ways?

Bildad the Shuhite offered that the rich and powerful are those who are good and right with God, while those who suffer must have done something to displease God. Perhaps Job was not as righteous and God-fearing as he had thought?

Zophar the Naamathite put it more plainly. "If iniquity is in your hand, remove it, and do not let injustice dwell in your tent" (Job 11:14).

As wealth and family were commonly understood as signs of God's blessings upon the righteous, his friends had added insult to his grievous loss and blackened his reputation. Job had lost his honor. He had nothing left to lose except his life.

With friends like these, Job's misery was complete.

Sometimes the best you can say to a friend in misery is nothing. Had Job's friends sat with him for seven days and seven nights in silence and left in silence, they would have in the least done no harm. It was not their place to defend God or to heal Job.

We can do better than Job's well-meaning friends. There are some things that you can say to a friend in misery. First, we will look at some of our common understandings of suffering. We will consider what the Church teaches about suffering and the cross. Finally, I will suggest some things you might say or not say to a suffering friend.

NINE MAXIMS OF SUFFERING

In my first year of priesthood, I came across a one-page list entitled, "Nine Maxims on Suffering." I showed the list to people who came to me with their suffering. While not the last word on the mystery of suffering, it became a way to talk about what they were going through. The way that the maxims are written captures our attempts to find meaning in suffering.

Nine Maxims of Suffering
by Cornie G. Remply

Suffering is not God's desire for us,
but occurs in the process of life.

Suffering is not given in order to teach us something,
but through it we learn.

Suffering is not given us to teach others something,
but through it they may learn.

Suffering is not given to punish us, but is sometimes
the consequence of sin or poor judgment.

Suffering does not occur because our faith is weak,
but through it our faith may be strengthened.

God does not depend on human suffering to achieve
God's purposes, but through it God's purposes are
sometimes achieved.

Suffering is not always to be avoided at all costs,
but is sometimes chosen.

Suffering can either destroy us or
add meaning to our life.

The will of God has more to do with how we
respond to life than with how life deals with us.

The author, I later discovered, was Reverend Cornel G. Rempel. He had been director of pastoral services and clinical pastoral education supervisor at Philhaven, Mt. Gretna, Pennsylvania. As a Mennonite pastor, hospital chaplain and supervisor of chaplains in training, he must have seen much suffering.

Let's walk through some of the maxims. Consider which one strikes you in particular as something you strongly agree with or disagree with.

Suffering is not God's desire for us, but occurs in the process of life.

"God did not make death, nor does he rejoice in the destruction of the living" (Wisdom 1:13). These words from the Book of Wisdom in the Old Testament make clear that God does not want us to suffer nor die. Just the opposite! Jesus said, "I came so that they might have life and have it more abundantly" (John 10:10).

Where does this idea come from that suffering is connected to God? Why do we so readily say, "It's God's plan," when God himself says, "No, it's not!"

Millions died in the Nazi concentration camps of World War II. Viktor Frankl survived. He noticed that some lived who were as starved and sick and tortured as many who died. He wondered why one person endured the brutality and indignation while a younger, stronger person did not.

Frankl discerned that the difference between life and death was not just physical treatment. It was the person's spiritual state.

His 1946 book, *Man's Search for Meaning,* paraphrased the philosopher Friedrich Nietzsche. "Those who have a 'why' to live, can bear with almost any 'how'." In other words, when you have purpose and meaning, you can endure great suffering.

The phrase, "It's God's will," is a well-intentioned way to give meaning to an otherwise meaningless car crash. We desperately want to believe that the world has purpose. We need to know that someone is in charge. We find strength in believing that there is a plan, however obscure it may be.

The Book of Wisdom would have you see it differently. "But by the envy of the devil, death entered the world" (Wisdom 2:24). In other words, suffering is not God's will. It's the devil's will! While God wants us to have life and have it more abundantly, the devil wants us to suffer and die.

Jesus came to show us God's true desire for us. He preached against the devil's lies. He proclaimed the Kingdom of God. His purpose was to overcome the powers that make us suffer and die. The Gospel of Mark shows us God's will in action.

For example, a woman who had suffered hemorrhages for twelve years stole behind Jesus in the crowd. When she touched Jesus' cloak, her flow of blood immediately dried up. She fell down before Jesus, who said to her, "Daughter, your faith has saved you. Go in peace and be cured of your affliction" (Mark 5:34). The power of the Lord defeated the power that oppressed the woman.

Next, Jesus took the hand of Jairus' dead daughter and said to her, "Little girl, I say to you, arise!" (Mark 5:41). Immediately, the girl of twelve arose and walked around, astounding everyone. The power of the Lord defeated the power that brought death to Jairus' daughter.

When the storm on the Sea of Galilee swamped the boat and the disciples were perishing, Jesus rebuked the wind and commanded the sea, "Quiet. Be still." The wind ceased and there was a great calm (Mark 4:36-42). The power of the Lord reigned even over the powers of creation.

The calming of the storm at sea, the healing of the woman with hemorrhages, and the raising of Jairus' daughter to life revealed God's true desire. With deeds louder than words, Jesus showed that in his life, death and resurrection, the kingdom of God has come.

On this side of the grave, there is suffering. It occurs in the process of life. But suffering is definitely not God's desire for us.

Suffering is not given in order to teach us something, but through it we learn.

Put your hand on a hot stove, you won't make the same mistake twice. Sleep in late too many times, you either set about to find a job that starts later in the day or you go to bed earlier.

Pain, believe it or not, can be a good thing. Pain can be a gift from God. It is God's way to tell us that something is wrong. The pain in a cut finger tells you that the bleeding needs attention now or things could get worse.

Suffering is not given in order to teach you something. Suffering is not God's desire for you.

But God did make you with nerves that hurt when cut. He made you with feelings that ache when hurt. He made you with empathy that feels the suffering of others. These are God-given gifts.

Through pain, you learn. You learn to protect your body from knives and hot stoves. You learn to make decisions that help you and others rather than hurt them. Pain makes us good students. You can learn your greatest lessons from your failures.

Just as suffering is not given to teach us a lesson, it is worth underscoring that suffering is not given to teach others a lesson.

Suffering is not given to punish us, but is sometimes the consequence of sin or poor judgment.

On the evening of June 17, 2015, Dylann Roof murdered Rev. Clementa C. Pinckney and eight members of the Emanuel African Methodist Episcopal Church in Charleston, South Carolina. After he had sat through a Bible study for an hour, he stated that he was there "to kill black people" and opened fire.

Before taking the lives of eight church members and their pastor, Roof had reportedly said, "You are raping our women and taking over the country." Earlier, Roof had himself photographed with the flags of the Confederacy, apartheid South Africa, and Rhodesia.[24]

Thirty-six years earlier, the U.S. Catholic Bishops had written, "Racism is a sin: a sin that divides the human family, blots out the image of God among specific members of that family, and violates the fundamental human dignity of those called to be children of the same Father. Racism is the sin that says some human beings are inherently superior and others essentially inferior because of races."[25]

Racism, the bishops wrote, mocks the words of Jesus who commanded us to treat others the way you would have them treat you. It violates his commandment to love our neighbor.

No one would say that those murdered in the Charleston church were being punished for something they had done. It was not a divine judgment on the Emanuel Church.

Instead, their suffering was in part the consequence of the sin of racism. "Killing black people" was justified by racism. The fruits of racism illustrate the maxim, "Suffering is sometimes the consequence of sin of others and society."

The maxim adds that suffering can also be the consequence of one's own poor judgment.

On the road one evening, I was stopped at an intersection. When the traffic light turned green, I put my car in gear but quickly stomped on the brakes. I had almost driven into a teenage girl. She was walking against the green light and talking into her cell phone. I honked my horn and called out, "Please be careful!" She looked up, shrugged, and continued walking against traffic and talking into her cell phone.

Her poor judgment to cross a six lane highway without looking where she was going nearly earned the teenager an ambulance ride to the hospital. Her suffering would not have been God's will. It would have been the result of her free will to walk and talk in traffic. Suffering is sometimes the consequence of poor judgment.

You can name for yourself examples that illustrate the soundness of the maxim, "Suffering is not given to punish us but is sometimes the consequence of sin or poor judgment." For example, the hundreds of thousands of deaths caused every year by smoking cigarettes are not a divine punishment. Death is simply a predictable consequence from smoking cigarettes.

Why then do we sometimes believe that suffering is a punishment from God?

Here's my guess. Parents discipline their children. It might be a time-out for five minutes in another room. It might be extra chores. The aim of the discipline is not to inflict pain. Discipline is to correct a certain behavior.

What parents call discipline, children call punishment. The time-out for five minutes is an eternity for a child. From a child's point-of-view, the extra chores are proof that their parents do not love them and want them to be miserable. It's not a big leap for our inner child to connect the consequences of sin and poor judgment with punishment from God.

The story of King David and Bathsheba gives us Scripture's understanding of sin, poor judgment, and divine punishment.

King David, as you might recall, was a famous king of Israel. He lusted after Bathsheba, the wife of his loyal soldier Uriah who was away fighting in the king's army, and took her to his bed. Later, Bathsheba sent word that she was pregnant.

To hush up her pregnancy, David brought Uriah home from the battlefield and wined and dined him. Yet Uriah, constant to his comrades in the field, refused to go home to his wife Bathsheba and instead slept on the palace floor. David sent him back to battle where he instructed his general to fall back and let Uriah be killed (2 Samuel 11:1-12:25).

One thing had led to another. David's lust led to the rape of Bathsheba, the murder of her husband, and the misuse of his power to cover up his evil deeds.

Nathan the prophet deftly exposed the cover-up. Rather than directly confront him, he posed a legal case for David to decide. David immediately judged, "The man who has done this deserves to die."

His sentence was his own death sentence. David, realizing that he was the one who deserved to die, repented. "I have sinned against the Lord."

Nathan said to him, "Now the Lord has put away your sin; you shall not die."

Although David was forgiven, his sins had consequences. The story does not have an entirely happy ending. The consequences of David's sin remained.

Uriah had been killed. David and Bathsheba's child died. Another son, Absalom, led a coup against David. Absalom's attempt to overthrow his father ended when David's general ran a sword through him.

The Lord forgave David. His guilt was forgiven. But his sin, as with every evil, had consequences. One can burn down a neighbor's house and later deeply regret the deed. The neighbor can even forgive the arsonist. But the house is still a smoldering ruin. Consequences persist even after the pardon.

Suffering is not given to punish us but is sometimes the consequence of sin or poor judgment.

The good news for David is that God limited the consequences. He even gave hope. The Lord gave David's family tree another chance.

A thousand years later, Joseph, a descendent from the House of David, became the husband of a woman with child. The child, rightly called the Son of David, was none other than God's own son, Jesus.

Suffering is not given to punish us but is sometimes the consequence of sin or poor judgment. Yet God's mercy has the last word.

God does not depend on human suffering to achieve God's purposes, but through it God's purposes are sometimes achieved.

Jim, a graduate from the University of Pennsylvania's Wharton School of Business, worked in corporate finance at General Electric for six years. Not happy with the corporate world, he decided to enter the Society of Jesus, commonly known as the Jesuits.

In the seminary studying for priesthood, Jim developed carpal tunnel syndrome. It was not life threatening. Others suffered much more than he did. Still, it was frustrating, unpredictable and sometimes painful.

He lamented to his spiritual director, "I don't want this cross!" He wanted to write books and articles. He wanted to type pain-free. He had great plans that did not include carpal tunnel syndrome.

His spiritual director answered, "Jim, it's hardly a cross if you want it!"

Jesus had said, "Amen, amen, I say to you, unless a grain of wheat falls to the ground and dies, it remains just a grain of wheat; but if it dies, it produces much fruit." Jesus taught in word and in action that whoever puts his own life above others loses it. Paradoxically, whoever gives his life for others saves it for eternal life (John 12:24-25).

Jim slowly came to understand that the part of his self that wanted to control his future had to be like a grain of wheat and die. It dawned upon him that everything he wrote was thanks to God's grace.

The insight freed him from the burden to control everything. Not able to make grand plans about his writing, he grew in humility. Curbed by carpal tunnel syndrome, he strove to write when he could and leave the rest to God.

Jim was ordained and became known as Father James Martin, a Jesuit priest. Father Martin has written nearly a dozen other books on spirituality, edited several books, and served as a commentator with diverse news agencies.[26]

There is a second way to look at this maxim, "... through suffering God's purposes are sometimes achieved." Besides the paradox how God's purposes can be achieved through our own sufferings, God's purposes can be achieved through the suffering of others.

In response to the massacre of forty-nine people at an Orlando nightclub on June 12, 2016, Orlando residents lined up to give blood. Millions of dollars from around the world flowed into a fund to assist victims and their families. The suffering of the victims and the community was horrific. As if in reply to the worst shooting massacre in U.S. history, the best in others was brought out.

Saint Pope John Paul II wrote a beautiful reflection, *On the Christian Meaning of Human Suffering*. He gave as example the story of the Good Samaritan. A Samaritan traveler who normally had nothing to do with Jews stopped to help a Jew who had been robbed, stripped, and beaten until half dead. The Samaritan bound up his wounds and took him to an inn, where he cared for him. Before continuing his journey, he gave money to the innkeeper to care for the victim and promised to repay him (Luke 10:29-37).

The Good Samaritan put into action the command of Jesus, "Love your neighbor." Going beyond sympathy and compassion, he freely gave his time, money and self for the suffering neighbor. John Paul II adds that society itself, in its medical institutions, education systems and social work is at its best structured on the example of the Good Samaritan.[27]

John Paul II draws from this reflection on the Christian meaning of human suffering the key insight that "suffering is present in the world in order to release love."[28] It elicits the best in us to be like the Good Samaritan.

The power of suffering to release love goes beyond the personal. It transforms "the whole of human civilization into a 'civilization of love'." The kingdom of God is the civilization of love proclaimed by Christ in his words and especially in his crucifixion.

At the Last Judgment, Christ reveals, "Whatever you did for one of these least brothers of mine, you did it for me" (Matthew 25:40). He is present in the suffering of the hungry, thirsty, naked, sick, and stranger, and they share in his sufferings that redeem the world. He receives the help of the Good Samaritan and at the same time he is the Good Samaritan who gave himself to save humanity from sin and death.

"At one and the same time Christ has taught man to do good by his suffering and to do good to those who suffer. In this double aspect he has completely revealed the meaning of suffering."[29] Simply put, suffering releases redeeming love.

Finally, God's purposes are always achieved. How and when, we do not always know. Sometimes suffering brings about his will. The cross is the ultimate instance of suffering achieving God's purposes. God does not depend on human suffering to achieve God's purposes, but through it God's purposes are sometimes achieved.

Suffering is not always to be avoided at all costs, but is sometimes chosen.

This is really important. Let's say it again. *Suffering is not always to be avoided at all costs, but is sometimes chosen.*

One graduation season I attended the high school graduation of a niece and another high school graduation of a nephew. Besides the colors of the robes, the two graduations followed the same script. The color guard brought in the flags. We stood and said the Pledge of Allegiance, ending with the inspirational, "... one nation, under God, with liberty and justice for all." The chorus sang, and then the speeches began.

The valedictorian speech encouraged the graduates to persevere, like a boulder in a river, not going with the current but standing your ground. A salutatorian speech told us to learn from our failures. Above all, the speeches exhorted us, "Follow your passion! Chart your own course! March to the beat of your own drummer!"

The speeches promised that the world is your oyster. "You can be whoever you want to be," the commencement speakers gushed, "when you make up your mind and do it."

The assumption behind these speeches was that when you follow your passion, you will be fulfilled and happy. That's the purpose of life, right?

This is an incomplete message at best. If this is the message you heard at your graduation, you did not hear enough. If this is what was said, you were cruelly misled.

What's missing in these speeches is mention of anyone else. Like a giant selfie, the graduates' future was all about their dreams, their hopes, their desires, and their hard work. There was no room left for anyone else.

Compare these speeches to a graduation speech given two thousand years ago.

The disciples, after the terrible events in Jerusalem where Jesus had been arrested, scourged, and lynched, and after the incredible news that Jesus had risen from the dead, returned home to Galilee.

On the Galilean mountaintop, a favorite place for them to gather in prayer, Jesus appeared to the disciples.

Resurrected from the dead and moments before ascending to heaven, Jesus gave his final words to his disciples. Like a graduation speech, he sent his followers into the world with these final instructions.

He said, "Go and make disciples." Period.

He did not say, "Go and fulfill yourself." He did not say, "Go and follow your bliss." He did not say, "Go and pursue happiness." He did not even raise the bar to "try to be kinder."

Jesus simply said, "Go and make disciples." In other words, "It is not about you."

The columnist David Brooks once observed, "Most people don't form a self and then lead a life. They are called by a problem, and the self is constructed gradually by their calling."

For example, a young woman, miserable from a dysfunctional boss, develops management skills so that the office can function. A mother, disturbed by the classroom misunderstandings of her son with Asperger's syndrome, joins the PTA to help the school administration better serve students such as her son. The sufferings of immigrants, the ill, and the vulnerable have inspired countless people to dedicate themselves to reforming our society to hold up human dignity and life.

The peace you seek is the fruit of serving others. Rather than to find yourself, the purpose of life is to lose yourself. Your calling is where your deep passion meets the world's deep need.

On Memorial Day, our nation remembers those who died in the service. They died in the service of others, not of themselves. They gave their lives in the service of liberty and justice for all.

We do not remember their courage, dreams, hopes, hard work, and perseverance, as worthy as these qualities are. We remember their sacrifice and their service that cost them their lives.

In a park in downtown Oviedo, Florida, hundreds of crosses stood at attention. Each cross was for a soldier from Florida who died in the wars in Afghanistan or Iraq. In the days leading up to the Memorial Day ceremony, people would quietly walk through the display of crosses, giving thanks for those who gave their lives for the cause of liberty and justice for all. Each cross was a reminder of a life given in sacrifice. Memorial Day remembered their sacrifice.

What was missing from the high school graduation speeches that I had heard was that one word, sacrifice.

Sacrifice by its nature is not for oneself. Sacrifice is freely chosen for others without regard to personal gain or cost.

Training for a 5K run, setting aside time three or four times a week to slip into gym shorts and a t-shirt, to walk and run and chant in sweaty breaths, "No pain, no gain," as you hustle the last lap, takes discipline. Discipline is a good thing, but it is not the same thing as sacrifice.

Working hard, putting in long hours, studying, and driving a beater so that one day you can have the new BMW and a big house, vacation on the beach in the summer and ski in the Rockies in the winter may be popularly considered sacrifice, but the correct term is delayed gratification. There is nothing inherently wrong with delayed gratification, but it is not the same thing as sacrifice.

Delayed gratification and discipline have their place, but in the end, they are not worth dying for. Neither are they worth living for.

Sacrifice is worth living for. Sacrifice by definition is doing something for others that costs you.

Pope Benedict wrote, "Truth and justice must stand above my comfort and physical well-being." Some things are more important than your own comfort. In fact, your discomfort is not an option if you want to love. "Love simply cannot exist without this painful renunciation of myself, in which I allow myself to be pruned and wounded, for otherwise it becomes pure selfishness and thereby ceases to be love."

Let me say a word to you parents, uncles, aunts, and grandparents who could not be more proud of your graduates: Please speak the truth.

If you say to them, "I don't care what work you do, just do whatever makes you happy," they will fill in the "whatever" blank with video games. They will restlessly pursue that white whale of their personal happiness and jump from job to job and relationship to relationship, misled by the fruitless pursuit of happiness. They will learn slowly or perhaps never at all that happiness happens on the way when you are serving others.

Ask them rather, "What do you want to do with your life?" If they vaguely mention, "Help others", encourage them, "Tell me more." Use graduation speeches to start a conversation. "The speaker talked about 'follow your dreams.' What do you think about that?" You might even dare to say, "What does the Lord want you to do?"

Our nation celebrates Memorial Day once a year, on the fourth Monday of May. For believers, however, every Sunday is Memorial Day.

Every Mass is a memorial. It is a memorial of the sacrifice of Jesus Christ. He gave his life for our sake. He died that we may live. More than his teachings and his life, we remember his death and resurrection.

The little crosses on the lawn in downtown Oviedo meant something because they shared in the great cross on Calvary, the altar of the body and blood of Jesus the Christ.

The end of the Mass is a mini-graduation. The priest says, "Go, and announce the Gospel of the Lord."

Go and make disciples. Baptize them into the one life where it is better to give than receive. Tell them not to be afraid to put God in the center instead of themselves. Show them in what you say and do and how you live, it's not about you. Show them that in dying to self they rise to life for others.

Show them how God our Father has pursued his passion and his passion is us. Tell them how he sent his son Jesus Christ who sacrificed everything for them and gave that graduation command, not a piece of advice but a single command, that bears the fruit of happiness, a command that life itself depends on.

"This is my commandment: love one another as I love you" (John 15:12).

"Suffering is not always to be avoided at all costs, but is sometimes chosen." Isn't that what Christ did? Isn't that what Christians do?

Suffering can either destroy us or add meaning to our life.

Close to a million Tutsis were killed in the spring of 1994. The Rwanda genocide rooted in the ethnic divisions among the Hutu, Tutsi and the Twa created untold widows and orphans, demolished homes, and left dead bodies everywhere. Dogs were turned on people. Women were raped, babies smashed on walls, families thrown into pit latrines, and mothers drowned in rivers.

In one particularly evil act in a country flooding in blood, a parish priest and a businessman ordered a bulldozer to demolish a church. Nearly all of the three thousand people taking refuge in the church were crushed. It was nine days after Easter Sunday 1994.[30]

The words of the prophet Habakkuk captured the suffering and despair. "How long, O LORD, must I cry for help and you do not listen? Or cry out to you, 'Violence!' and you do not intervene?" (Habakkuk 1:2).

The parents and many of the relatives of Marcel Uwineza were killed in the genocide. His grief however did not destroy him. Instead, he changed.

"One day I met one of the killers of my brothers and sister. Upon seeing me, he came toward me. I thought he was coming to kill me too. But I could not believe what happened. As if in a movie, he knelt before me and asked me to forgive him. After a time of confusion, asking myself what was happening, and by a force which I could not describe, I took him, embraced him and said: 'I forgive you; the Lord has been good to me.' Ever since that moment, I have felt free."[31]

Giving forgiveness healed Uwineza. He came to understand how his suffering profoundly related him to God. A desire grew in him to give himself to the Lord as a Jesuit priest. Through his wounds he was able to help those wounded in the struggle and dwelling in darkness to seek reconciliation and salvation. He offered hope "based on the love of God for everyone: rich and poor, black and white, gay and straight, Jew and Arab, Palestinian and Israeli, Serb and Albanian, Hutu and Tutsi, Pakistani and Indian – none are outside the purview of God's love."

Suffering did not destroy Marcel Uwineza. Instead, through the grace of forgiveness, it changed him. Suffering gave birth to his priesthood. It gave meaning to his life.

Our suffering can either destroy us or add meaning to our life.

In the midst of suffering, we tend to run away or be strong. We take flight or stand to fight. We try to figure out God's plan.

The final answer to suffering is the response that God himself has given. God did not fight suffering with armies. He did not flee suffering and stay safe in heaven. In his suffering on the cross, Jesus Christ embraced evil and covered it with forgiveness. Vengeance gave way to mercy.

Marcel Uwineza discovered it in the encounter with the killer of his brothers and sister. Like Father Uwineza, suffering can add meaning to your life. It might change you so that you become a priest helping others in their suffering. Suffering can make you more understanding and compassionate. While water runs off a stone, grace can enter a broken heart.

Suffering can either destroy us or add meaning to our life.

Do Not Be Afraid of Suffering.

When the person you pray with asks, "Why me?" or "Where is God?", he or she is not asking for a theological presentation on suffering. They are crying out from a broken heart that needs above all your love. They do not care what you know until they know that you care. Prayer and compassion is your first and best response.

Only after you have listened to them and offered a prayer, you might have an opportunity to nudge them to consider another perspective. The nine maxims and Pope John Paul II's reflections might give you a way to offer the Christian meaning of suffering.

Job's friends tried to comfort him in his misery. We can learn from their example some things not to say:

- "It's God's plan." Suffering is not God's plan. God's plan is to save us from sin, not to afflict us.

- "Maybe Lord has answered and you just aren't listening." This could be true; it could also be blaming the victim.

- "Maybe the answer was No." Or similarly, "Maybe you are not asking for the right thing or in the right way." Again, this could be true; it could also be blaming the victim.

- "Maybe the Lord will answer the prayer, only in God's time. After all, when the Scripture says that the door will open, it does not promise *when* the door will open." This bromide puts some responsibility on God. Still, it is cold comfort to a person who is hanging on for dear life to faith in a caring Father.

While these explanations are logically possible, they do not square with a loving Father who gives good things to his children. They sound more like a defense of God's inexplicable silence than a profession of faith in his mercy.

Some things you can say:

- "I don't know what to say." It's okay to say that you don't have the answers. Mary stood at the foot of the cross of her son Jesus, without answers and powerless to do anything for him (John 19:25). Yet her fearless and faithful presence must have said more than a thousand words. Your willingness to share in the powerlessness of another is an act of love.

- "How can I help?" This question usually does not have an immediate answer, but it shows your willingness to go beyond a dismissive pat on the back.

- "What would you like to pray for?" As mentioned earlier, this question invites the person to name what is on their heart. It opens the way to lift them up to the Lord in prayer.

Like Father Uwineza, your own suffering joined to the cross of Christ helps you to go beyond clichés and offer a truly healing word from the Lord. Trust your suffering in Christ to guide you.

For Discussion

- Which of the Nine Maxims of Suffering do you strongly agree with? Which do you disagree with?

- "John Paul II draws from this reflection on the Christian meaning of human suffering the key insight that 'suffering is present in the world in order to release love.'" *When in your life has suffering "released love"? When has it not? What was the difference?*

- When was a time that someone comforted you in your suffering? What did they say and do?

CONCLUSION

THE GAP BETWEEN ASKING AND ANSWER

A friend shares their troubles. Your response this time is to do more than offer sympathy. You work up the nerve to go out on a long, thin limb and offer, "Can I say a prayer with you?"

You place a hand on their shoulder and lift up your eyes to heaven. "Lord, your Spirit raised Jesus from the dead. We give thanks for your power. Send your Spirit upon your servant N. Please raise him to new life. Through Christ our Lord. Amen."

And then nothing happens. No healing. No sense of peace. No clue what to do next. Like a firework fizzling, the moment passes as if it never happened.

We pray and pray, yet often nothing happens. How do we reconcile seemingly unanswered prayer with Scripture such as, "And we have this confidence in him, that if we ask anything according to his will, he hears us. And if we know that he hears us in regard to whatever we ask, we know that what we have asked him for is ours" (1 John 5:14-15)?

At the Last Supper, Jesus left us these encouraging words, "And whatever you ask in my name, I will do, so that the Father may be glorified in the Son." He added, "If you ask anything of me in my name, I will do it" (John 14:13–14). Jesus could not have said it more simply. Ask him, and he will do it.

Jesus taught us to be persistent in our prayer. He gave the example of the man who went to his neighbor at midnight to ask for three loaves of bread for an unexpected visitor. Jesus' point was that if the neighbor does not get out of bed out of friendship, he will get out of bed and hand over the loaves of bread just to get some sleep!

Surely God will treat you better than that neighbor at midnight. Jesus concludes the little story with a seemingly clear-cut promise. "And I tell you, ask and you will receive; seek and you will find; knock and the door will be opened to you. For everyone who asks, receives; and the one who seeks, finds; and to the one who knocks, the door will be opened" (Luke 11:9-10).

Only, that is not our experience. Who has not doggedly asked, sought and knocked, yet did not receive, did not find, and the door did not open? Who needs three loaves of bread? You would be happy to settle for half a loaf.

Ask, seek, knock – and sometimes there is no answer. The gap between asking and answer is as wide as the Grand Canyon. Nothing happens. All our persistence in prayer does not open the door. The bread we desperately need does not appear. Sometimes we go hungry.

We began this little book with Jesus in the Garden of Gethsemane where he knelt in agonizing prayer. Soon he would be arrested, beaten, and crucified. His own prayer for this cup to be taken from him was not granted.

The next day, Good Friday, he would be executed and buried in a tomb.

Then something happened. No one had expected it. No one could explain it. Early in the morning on the third day, the day we now know as Easter Sunday, the tomb was found empty.

Christ appeared to Mary Magdalene, then to the apostles and to more disciples. At first they did not recognize him. He had changed. Even more amazingly, something in the world had changed.

He did not do what might be expected of an innocent man put to death. Risen from the dead, Jesus did not seek vengeance on the Roman soldiers. Pontius Pilate, the Roman governor who gave him over to the mob, did not meet with a mysterious death. The religious leaders who persecuted him remained as religious leaders.

Risen from the dead, Jesus Christ did not seek vengeance. Nor did he triumphantly prove that he was right. He did not even go back to doing what he had done before. He did not preach the kingdom of God. He did not heal the sick and cure lepers.

Instead, he commissioned those who believed in him to go and do what he had begun. Giving them on Pentecost his own Spirit, the Lord sent his followers to teach about the kingdom of God, heal the sick, and cure lepers. They were to love God and neighbor as Christ loved them even to the cross. They were to pray with others.

Following him did not protect them from suffering. He had told his followers, "Whoever wishes to come after me must deny himself, take up his cross, and follow me." The cross was part of following Christ. The mystery of suffering shared in the life of Christ.

In the end, the final answer to our prayers is the mystery of the cross. The petitions give way to the cross and resurrection. Like Jesus Christ in the Garden of Gethsemane entering into his passion, we pray, "Your will be done."

He is risen. He is praying for you right now. At the right hand of God the Father, he is our high priest interceding for us.

And so you can pray with the power of the Holy Spirit, "Your will be done," and add, "Through Christ our Lord. Amen."

RESOURCES FOR YOUR PRAYER LIFE

You might be glad to know that there are many excellent books and websites to help you grow in your prayer life.

Magnificat and *Give Us This Day* are Catholic prayer books for daily personal and liturgical prayer. Through a monthly subscription, you receive a pocket-size prayer book with the scripture readings for daily and Sunday Mass, as well as hymns, art, spiritual writings, modern reflections, and the stories of the saints. I use my copy daily to pray and to prepare the next day's homily.

Give Us This Day is published by Liturgical Press, a ministry of the monks of St. John's Abbey in Collegeville, Minnesota. You can get print or online versions at *www.giveusthisday.org*. *Magnificat* is available in English, Spanish, and French. You can find out more at *http://www.magnificat.net/*.

One of the great treasures of the Church for prayer is the daily praying of the Psalms known as the Liturgy of the Hours. Also known as the Breviary or the Divine Office, the Liturgy of the Hours is the official Church handbook for daily prayer. The term "Hours" refers to the fact that the prayers are at set times, or hours, through the day. You can pray each "Hour" in ten or fifteen minutes. Long before Islam had the practice to pause five times a day to pray, Christianity has had this custom to praise God through the day.

Besides making the promises of celibacy and obedience, the Catholic clergy promise to pray the Liturgy of the Hours daily. At their ordination, deacons and priests are asked, "Are you resolved to maintain and deepen a spirit of prayer appropriate to your way of life and, in keeping with what is required of you, to celebrate faithfully the Liturgy of the Hours for the Church and for the whole world?"

If the Liturgy of the Hours is that important and valuable for bishops, priests and deacons, imagine if Catholics praised God not only during Mass on Sunday but also Monday through Saturday in the morning, afternoon, and evening. The Church highly encourages everyone, clergy and laity, to pray the Liturgy of the Hours.

You can get a free app for the Liturgy of the Hours at sites such as *www.universalis.com*, *www.divine-office.com*, and *www.ibreviary.com*. Some are audio and some are in various languages. As the Liturgy of the Hours can be intimidating, you might get a guidebook such as *The Everyday Catholic's Guide to the Liturgy of the Hours* by Daria Sockey. The U.S. bishops' website *www.usccb.org/prayer-and-worship/liturgy-of-the-hours/index.cfm* gives a short overview of the Hours.

The prayer from your heart is more than good enough, but sometimes it helps to have a model. *Catholic*

Household Blessings and Prayers offers prayers and blessings for all occasions such as birth and adoption, childhood, marriage, sickness or infirmity, and death and grief. "Whether in times of joy or times of grief, God is always with us."

It has a section of basic prayers that you might commit to memory and teach your children and grandchildren. There are prayers for the Church and the World on topics such as Christian unity, the culture of life, evangelization and missions, leaders in the church and community, migrants and refugees, peace, persons with disabilities, social justice, and victims of abuse. *Part VIII, God's Word in Times of Need* leads you to scripture passages on issues such as anger, forgiveness, love, quiet, trouble, crisis, and conflict.

Published by the U.S. bishops and bound in leather, consider giving it as a wedding gift, on the occasion of a birth or to a friend moving into a new home.

My adult prayer life owes a debt to monks. After graduating from the university, I spent a month at a monastery in Rhode Island to discern if I was a monk. In two weeks' time, I knew that I was not a monk. They went to church five times a day! The kicker was when two of us monastic visitors took a free afternoon to go the movies. We walked down the dark aisle of the movie theater, genuflected, and took our seats. Thank goodness the darkened movie theater hid our force of habit.

My month-long monastic immersion gave me the habit of daily prayer. A day does not pass when I do not spend several periods of prayer, at least twenty minutes each, to praise God and pray for others. I wish that everyone could take a month at a monastery to gain the habit of daily prayer. If you cannot, you should treat yourself to at least a weekend retreat.

I was further blessed by my five years of seminary formation at St. Meinrad Seminary in Indiana. Founded by the monks of St. Meinrad Archabbey, the seminary was infused with their spirit of prayer. The way of life of the Benedictine monks, following the rule of St. Benedict, is summed up in "Ora et Labora" which means "prayer and work." The monks of St. Meinrad Archabbey wrote a collection of essays on prayer, its history, and the Church liturgy. Their book *The Tradition of Catholic Prayer* is published by Liturgical Press at *www.litpress.org*.

Much of *Can I Say a Prayer With You?* is about intercessory prayer. Sister Ann Shields has written two friendly books about intercessory prayer.

The book *Intercession: A Guide to Effective Prayer* is a Bible study. If you were inspired by the story of how Abraham interceded for Sodom, you can learn how Ezekiel, Jeremiah and Jesus stood in the gap for the people, and how Moses and Daniel pleaded for mercy on behalf of the people. The book is a guide to study scripture individually and with a group.

Pray and Never Lose Heart: The Power of Intercession is not so much a how-to book as a who-prays book. Sister Ann reflects on how one becomes a person of prayer and an intercessor. Christ is the vine, we are the branches, and God the Father prunes us so that "those who see us might see Jesus."

The Nativity scene in your home during Christmas time, ashes on Ash Wednesday and palms on Palm Sunday are blessings that make holy certain times and places. Bells, candles, holy oils, holy water, statues and medals surround us with sacred signs of faith and help us to pray. The book *Amazing Graces: The Blessings of Sacramentals* by Julie Dortch Cragon gives you the history and spirituality of the sacramentals. It explains how sacramentals make tangible the sense of God in your home and your daily life.

My hope has been to offer encouragement so that you would pray often and faithfully with others in their need. May these gifts help you become a person of prayer and ever more able to say, "Can I say a prayer with you?"

ACKNOWLEDGMENTS

They say that if you want to go fast, go alone. If you want to go far, go together.

This book is thanks to many going together with me: Mary Dall for the illustrations, Rev. Randy Greenwald for friendship and pastoral insight, Bert Ghezzi for editing and encouragement, Eileen LoFaso for proofreading, Tim Schoenbachler for book layout and technical support, and my sister Theresa Degler for the cover background.

The faithful who have shared their stories of prayer, some included in these pages, have helped me to appreciate the truth of "where two or three are gathered together in my name. . . ."

I am grateful for those who have formed me into a person of prayer. Besides the monks of St. Meinrad Archabbey in Indiana, the wisdom and holiness of retreat masters and spiritual directors, especially Jaime Madrid and Dick Dunphy, have been my guides. Prayer, like love, is caught. May the Lord reward them for their labors.

ENDNOTES

[1] I am grateful to Randy Greenwald for this insight.

[2] It gets better. When we don't know what to say or how to pray, the Holy Spirit is praying for us too! "In the same way, the Spirit too comes to the aid of our weakness; for we do not know how to pray as we ought, but the Spirit itself intercedes with inexpressible groanings….for the holy ones according to God's will" (Romans 8:26-27).

[3] "Joe" is not his real name. In this book, I changed the names and details of some stories to protect the identity of people. The stories with real names use their full name.

[4] Sister Briege McKenna with Henry Libersat, *Miracles Do Happen* (Ann Arbor, Michigan: Servant Books, 1987), 4-5.

[5] Based on an interview on March 9, 2016.

[6] Rick Caldwell, from a homily given July 24, 2015 at Saint Meinrad School of Theology.

[7] Francis MacNutt, *The Practice of Healing Prayer: A How-To Guide For Catholics* (Frederick, Maryland: The Word Among Us Press, 2010), 66-70.

[8] Father Prentice Tipton suggests, after listening to someone in distress, simply stating, "When these things happen in my life, this is where my faith makes a difference." You don't have to say anything else. They may ask to hear more. They may not. You've opened a door to them to walk through. Chapel Chat, July 2016, Our Lady of Good Counsel. *https://www.youtube.com/watch?v =Ava0gyiDVNs.* Retrieved August 9, 2016.

[9] The promise of the covenant was realized when Abraham became the father of faith for the three great monotheistic religions: Judaism, Christianity, and Islam. When we sing the children's song, "Father Abraham had many sons, and many sons had father

Abraham," this covenant is what we are singing about. The family tree of these three religions shares one ancestor in faith, Abraham.

[10]A year later, the three visitors would have the last laugh. Sarah and Abraham gave birth to a son, Isaac, as they had been promised. Isaac had a son, Jacob. The twelve sons of Jacob, who was also known as Israel, became the founding fathers of the twelve tribes of Israel, but that is another story.

[11]In Scripture, "Sodom and Gomorrah" was a shorthand reference for sinful cities. They were the ancient version of modern-day Las Vegas. Their sins, though, were not gambling, prostitution, and organized crime. Isaiah 1:9–10; 3:9 sees the sin of Sodom and Gomorrah as injustice against the orphan and widow, the weak and powerless. Ezekiel 16:46–51 compares Sodom and Gomorrah to those complacent in prosperity while giving no help to the poor and needy. Jeremiah 23:14 condemns Sodom and Gomorrah for adultery, idolatry, and strengthening the power of the wicked. In the Genesis story, the sin of Sodom is violation of the sacred duty of hospitality. Abraham and Sarah had given their guests rest, refreshment and a feast. The people of Sodom, in violent contrast, sought to rape the three visitors who had become Lot's guests.

[12]The question, "Did Abraham change the Lord's mind?" is not a question that the story was trying to answer. The story was told to show us that the mercy of God is greater than our justice. Exactly how prayer for others works is a mystery. What is important to know is that prayer for others does work. Jesus had promised, "If you then, who are wicked, know how to give good gifts to your children, how much more will your heavenly Father give good things to those who ask him" (Matthew 7:11). Just as he wants us to live, God the Father wanted the people of Sodom to live. His desire for our salvation never changes. His love for us is unchanging.

[13]The Rays won the baseball game in a gripping come-from-behind finish.

[14]"St Maximilian Kolbe: Priest Hero of a Death Camp." *http://www.catholic-pages.com/saints/st_maximilian.asp.* Retrieved July 21, 2016.

[15]St. Francis of Assisi was the first person known to receive the stigmata. Since then, dozens of saints have been known to bear the marks of Christ. My parish, Most Precious Blood Catholic Church, has named some of its meeting rooms after stigmatic saints: St. Catherine of Sienna, St. Faustina, and St. Francis.

[16]Diane Allen, *Pray, Hope, and Don't Worry: True Stories of Padre Pio, Book 1* (San Diego, California: Padre Pio Press, 2012), 401.

[17]Ibid., 328.

[18]*http://padrepiodevotions.org/testimonials/.* The testimonies were submitted through the internet. They are not known to have been authenticated. Retrieved July 21, 2016.

[19]"The testimony of Mrs. Sanita Maria Lucia Ippolito on The Miracle." Published in February 2002, Voce di Padre Pio, the official magazine for the cause of Padre Pio and published by Padre Pio's Friary in San Giovanni Rotondo. *http://www.sanpadrepio.com/Matteo.htm.* Retrieved July 20, 2016.

[20]Pope Francis visits the School "Our Lady Queen of the Angels" and meets children and families of immigrants in New York, from Harlem, on the occasion of his apostolic visit to the United States. *https://www.youtube.com/watch?v=e_B3CJ7dHc4.* Retrieved July 21, 2016.

[21]*Meeting with Children and Immigrant Families: Address of the Holy Father.* Our Lady Queen of Angels School, Harlem, New York. Friday, 25 September 2015. *http://w2.vatican.va/content/francesco/en/speeches/2015/september/documents/papa-francesco_20150925_usa-harlem.html.* Retrieved July 21, 2016.

[22]*Apostolic Blessing "Urbi Et Orbi": First Greeting Of The Holy Father Pope Francis.* Central Loggia of St. Peter's Basilica. Wednesday, 13 March 2013. *http://w2.vatican.va/content/francesco/en/speeches/2013/march/documents/papa-francesco_20130313_benedizione-urbi-et-orbi.html.* Retrieved July 21, 2016.

[23]These stories are slightly edited from private correspondence received August 1-2, 2016.

[24]Eric Foner, "The Historical Roots of Dylann Roof's Racism," posted June 25, 2015 in *The Nation. http://www.thenation.com/article/210817/historical-roots-dylann-roofs-racism.* Retrieved July 21, 2016.

[25]*Brothers And Sisters To Us, U.S. Catholic Bishops Pastoral Letter on Racism,* 1979. *http://www.usccb.org/issues-and-action/cultural-diversity/african-american/brothers-and-sisters-to-us.cfm.* Retrieved August 3, 2016.

[26]Father James Martin wrote the book *My Life with the Saints,* named by Publishers Weekly as one of the "Best Books of the Year" and mentioned in the earlier chapter on the Saints.

[27]John Paul II, *Apostolic Letter Salvifici Doloris,* ("On the Christian Meaning of Human Suffering", 1984), 29. *https://w2.vatican.va/content/john-paul-ii/en/apost_letters/1984/documents/hf_jp-ii_apl_11021984_salvifici-doloris.html.* Retrieved August 3, 2016.

[28]Ibid., 30.

[29]Ibid., 30.

[30]Three years after the main genocide, militiamen attacked the high school across the road from the bulldozed church. They demanded that the students separate along ethnic lines. In a shining moment, the students stood together, saying, "We are Rwandans." The militia attacked and many students were killed.

[31]Marcel Uwineza, "On Christian Hope," in *America,* April 4, 2016, 24-27.